AF545248

The Software Factory

Books and Training Products From QED

Database

- Migrating to DB2
- DB2: The Complete Guide to Implementation and Use
- DB2 Design Review Guidelines
- DB2: Maximizing Performance of Online Production Systems
- Embedded SQL for DB2: Application Design and Programming
- SQL for DB2 and SQL/DS Application Developers
- Using DB2 to Build Decision Support Systems
- The Data Dictionary: Concepts and Uses
- Logical Data Base Design
- Entity-Relationship Approach to Logical Data Base Design
- Database Management Systems: Understanding and Applying Database Technology
- Database Machines and Decision Support Systems: Third Wave Processing
- IMS Design and Implementation Techniques
- Repository Manager/MVS: Concepts, Facilities and Capabilities
- How to Use ORACLE SQL*PLUS
- ORACLE: Building High Performance Online Systems
- ORACLE Design Review Guidelines
- Using ORACLE to Build Decision Support Systems

Systems Engineering

- Effective Methods of EDP Quality Assurance
- Handbook of Screen Format Design
- Managing Software Projects: Selecting and Using PC-Based Project Management Systems
- The Complete Guide to Software Testing
- A User's Guide for Defining Software Requirements
- A Structured Approach to Systems Testing
- Storyboard Prototyping: A New Approach to User Requirements Analysis
- The Software Factory: Managing Software Development and Maintenance
- Data Architecture: The Information Paradigm
- Advanced Topics in Information Engineering
- Software Engineering with Formal Software Metrics

Management

- Introduction to Data Security and Control
- CASE: The Potential and the Pitfalls

Management (cont'd)

- Strategic and Operational Planning for Information Services
- Information Systems Planning for Competitive Advantage
- How to Automate Your Computer Center: Achieving Unattended Operations
- Ethical Conflicts in Information and Computer Science, Technology, and Business
- Mind Your Business: Managing the Impact of End-User Computing
- Controlling the Future: Managing Technology-Driven Change

Data Communications

- Data Communications: Concepts and Solutions
- Designing and Implementing Ethernet Networks
- Network Concepts and Architectures
- Open Systems: The Guide to OSI and its Implementation

IBM Mainframe Series

- QMF: How to Use Query Management Facility with DB2 and SQL/DS
- DOS/VSE: Introduction to the Operating System
- DOS/VSE: CICS Systems Programming
- DOS/VSE/SP Guide for Systems Programming: Concepts, Programs, Macros, Subroutines
- Advanced VSE System Programming Techniques
- Systems Programmer's Problem Solver
- VSAM: Guide to Optimization and Design
- MVS/JCL: Mastering Job Control Language
- MVS/TSO: Mastering CLISTS
- MVS/TSO: Mastering Native Mode and ISPF
- REXX in the TSO Environment

Video

- DB2: Building Online Production Systems for Maximum Performance
- Data Architecture: An Information Systems Strategy (Video)
- Building Online Production Systems with ORACLE 6.0
- Practical Data Modeling

Programming

- C Language for Programmers
- VAX/VMS: Mastering DCL Commands and Utilities

This is Only a Partial Listing. For Additional Information or a Free Catalog contact

QED Information Sciences, Inc. • P. O. Box 82-181 • Wellesley, MA 02181
Telephone: 800-343-4848 or 617-237-5656 or fax 617-235-0826

The Software Factory

Second Edition

Managing Software Development and Maintenance

James R. Johnson

QED Information Sciences, Inc.
Wellesley, Massachusetts • Montreal

P.O. Box 82-181
Wellesley, MA 02181

Library of Congress Catalog Number: 90-49429
International Standard Book Number: 0-89435-348-9

Printed in the United States of America
91 92 93 10 9 8 7 6 5 4 3 2

Library of Congress Cataloging-in-Publication Data

Johnson, James R.
The software factory : managing software development and maintenance / James R. Johnson.—2nd ed.
p. cm.
Includes index.
ISBN 0-89435-348-9
1. Computer software—Development—Management. I. Title.
QA76.76.D47J65 1991
005.1—dc20 90-49429
CIP

Contents

Foreword

Over the past 30 years a major new set of managerial challenges has been created by the rapid evolution and spread of information system technology. This evolution has provided a number of firms with the means to become more effective competitors by creatively using this technology. As a result, a significant focus on strategic and competitive uses of Information Technology (IT) dominates the literature. However, the effort required to actually implement these systems was vastly underestimated by many professionals.

The challenge of implementation has shown that many managers moved so stolidly toward engaging senior management and pursuing strategic/competitive use of technology, they moved away from some of the fundamentals of managing software development. Many IT managers face significant problems since their first hand technical experience was with technology so different from that of the 1980s. Further, the understanding of what makes acceptable management practice in the IT field has changed dramatically. Virtually all current conventional wisdom on management of this activity has been introduced in the last ten years. This places a special burden on IT management to not just address the day-to-day operating problems, but to also identify, assimilate and implement very different methods and approaches. If managers are not committed to a process of self-renewal they will become obsolete.

This book concentrates on effective management of IT resources with heavy emphasis on practical insights for delivering and maintaining high quality software systems. It provides a unique opportunity to examine, in depth, contemporary management of an IT activity.

The Software Factory is for professionals written by an outstanding professional. Jim's years of experience clearly come through in the hard-hitting, insightful chapters. He has developed an integrated view of IT management from a perspective of the late 1980s. Given the depth of factual and practical information on the software development and maintenance activity, I think you will find this an unusually helpful book.

James I. Cash, Jr.
Professor of Business Administration
Harvard Graduate School of Business Administration

Preface

Having worked in a Software Factory for 16 years and having managed the area for seven, it is satisfying to document our software development approach. In 1980, QED published my previous book titled *Managing For Productivity In Data Processing*. When requested to update the material, I realized that so much had changed over the years, a revision was impractical.

Thus, a new book resulted with a focused objective, managing a "factory," a factory producing business application software. It was not an introductory text; the book, published in 1989, was intended for professionals working in the MIS field who have practical experience in software development.

In the Information Technology industry, the rate of change is not slowing down. CASE, cooperative processing, business process redesign, Unix for business—all concepts evolving and changing the MIS environment. To address new issues, a number of major changes have been made for the 1991 edition:

- The three Strategic Business Planning (BSP) chapters are now Part I. Extensive new material in chapter one provides comments on the latest approaches.
- A new chapter four, on both upper and lower CASE, starts Part II. Additional appendices (D—limitations of Data Base Planning

and E—lower CASE concepts) provide supporting CASE material.

- Measurement data in Part III was updated (1989 versus 1987) along with factory statistics in Appendix A. Measurement calculations were placed in Appendix F to improve the readability of chapter seven.
- A new chapter eight on Quality was added to Part III relating the Japanese JIT approach to software quality.
- Part VIII contains a new chapter eighteen on managing the Data Center utility.
- And finally, other chapters were updated when appropriate.

James R. Johnson
Director of Data Center
Hallmark Cards, Inc.

Acknowledgements

This book resulted from the efforts of eight Systems Development Managers at Hallmark Cards, Inc., who were dedicated to improving the software development process. In fact, the same team of managers were together for seven years. Thus, credit for the organization's productivity and the concepts documented in this book goes to the team: Lavon Faught, Bob Fisher, Lynne Haler, Roy Henrich, Harold Lundy, Jim McDonald, Ron Smith, and Pete Thorsell. Each manager was involved in the implementation of one or more of the productivity concepts in this organization.

A Software Factory doesn't function in a vacuum. Our vice president, John Collins, provided support and consistent direction over the years. Also, the supporting technical departments helped us realize productivity with subsecond response time and software tools.

I would like to thank my secretary, Charlene Gill, for tolerating my constant revisions. Her talent for reading, correcting, and typing the material was invaluable.

The artwork was created by Susan Johnson.

Introduction

PERSPECTIVE

Over the past ten years, our organization has pursued productivity techniques for the Systems Development function. This book highlights what was learned, from Business System Planning (BSP) to counting Lines of Code (LOC). Our Systems Development department is a Software Factory, over two hundred professionals generating between 40 and 60 products per year, each with the following average characteristics:

Man Days	400–450
LOC	35,000
Function Points	300–400

The emphasis, varying from year to year, depended on new technology or areas of opportunity. For example, consider the major issues explored in the past nine years: 1990—Strategic Systems and Re-engineering; 1989—Upper Case Tools and Joint Application Design (JAD); 1988—Expert Systems Research; 1987—Code Generators; 1986—Performance Measurement and Third-Generation Language (3GL) Productivity; 1985—Technology Scan; 1984—Fourth-Generation Languages (4GL); 1983—Prototyping, Response Time Study; 1982—Function Points, Information Center.

Our conclusions have been validated by publishing articles in popular periodicals or speaking at MIS conferences. Comparing internal strategies to external sources, obtained passively through reading periodicals and books and attending conferences, or obtained actively by writing articles or presentations, assured a rational approach.

A FACTORY

Typically, Computer Operations is visualized as a factory, the computer processing thousands of jobs per day. However, the term *Software Factory*, in the context of this book, applies to the manufacture of programs, more specifically, programming system products or documented, integated business applications (as originally defined by Fred Brooks). Our term for this product is a *production system*, which requires "creator independence," allowing end-user modification for routine operation via tables or parameters.

Appendix A contains eight years of statistics on the factory's output. The base information includes Lines of Code, programs, program bugs (Unusual Conditions Reports, UCRs), projects' schedule and budget performance, Function Points, and staffing levels.

IMPORTANCE

Recent renewed interest in the Software Factory is based on two factors—one positive, one negative. Using technology as a competitive weapon generally requires strategic on-line systems; thus, management turns to the factory for implementation. On the negative side, visibility of high maintenance costs has top management concerned.

Also, as new technology (electronic mail, local area networks, personal computers, departmental computers, teleconferencing, cooperative processing, imaging, fax, voice response, etc.) proliferates, the implementation of systems has become more complex based on additional integration. Thus, managing a corporation's Software Factory will always be a priority subject.

ENVIRONMENT

One not necessarily intuitive observation learned from interfacing with other companies is that organizational environment and cultural differences are as important as technological considerations when selecting productivity techniques. The management priorities for a factory depend on both MIS and corporate characteristics, such factors as the technical stage of automation and the amount of end-user data processing activity.

Although software factories produce similar products, factory profiles vary considerably, directly reflecting the corporate environment/culture. The description of our organization in Appendix B provides the reader perspective and allows comparisons of organizational and environmental factors. The comments are not extensive; the intent is to convey a "flavor" of the environment.

MAINTENANCE

The contents of the book reflect what was important to improving both development and maintenance productivity in our "factory". Two-thirds of the book is devoted to managing the development process. However, chapters applying to both maintenance and development are:

4	CASE Strategies
7	Measuring Performance
8	Quality and JIT
10	Job Rotation
13	Response Time and Availability
15	Hardware/Software Tools
16	Test Plans

The statistics in Appendix A were used to compute maintenance productivity as defined in Chapter 7.

ORGANIZATION

The book is organized in seven parts, each with a central theme. Business System Planning (BSP) is a logical starting point since an organization must be working on the corporation's strategic systems to be effective. BSP is followed by directional tools, measurement, motivation, project management, the weakest link (availability and response time), productivity tools, and managing the utility. Although the book is focused, some topics have been slighted, such as recruiting and organization. These topics are important, but are unique to a corporate environment. Stating the questions answered in each part clarifies their content.

Part I Business System Planning (BSP)

Are corporate priorities reflected in the MIS portfolio?
Is top management involved in MIS planning?
What are the alternative methodologies?
What is a strategic system?

Part II Directional Tools

Why the paradox of different 4GL strategies?
Is CPU consumption the critical factor?
Does complexity influence language strategy?
What is Upper Case, Lower Case?
How should CASE be implemented?
Are code generators the future?
Will the factory adopt Expert Systems?

Part III Measurement

What are productivity measures?
Do the same measures apply, at different organizational levels, to the programmer analyst?
Is it possible to quantify total performance?
How much detail is enough?
Can Japanese Just In Time principles apply?

Part IV Motivation

Is burnout real?
Are performance reviews a positive experience?

Part V Projects

What basic steps apply to all projects?
Can steps be skipped?
Does an advanced procedure exist?
Are function points superior to lines of code?

Part VI The Weakest Link

Is subsecond response time cost-effective?
Does programmer productivity improve if response time is reduced from .5 seconds to .3, or from .3 to .2?
How should service-level agreements be monitored?

Part VII Productivity Tools

Why does prototyping apply?
Does cloning code improve productivity?
Do bullpens improve productivity?
Will audits improve quality?
Can testing be planned?

Part VIII Managing the Utility

What techniques help manage a data center?
Are vendor meetings required?
What are the Critical Success Factors in a data center?

The writing approach varies considerably among chapters: four, five and eighteen involve dialogue; six, nine and fourteen start with a quiz; and sixteen and seventeen are primarily examples. This variety should provide a change of pace while maintaining readability. Major references are included after selected chapters.

PART I

Business System Planning (BSP)

In theory, Business System Planning (BSP) is a straightforward, three-step activity: define needs, select an implementation strategy, and budget. In practice, executing the three steps successfully challenges the best management teams. Top management commitment, line management involvement (versus a planning department), innovative thinking, and a structure, including tools, are the keys to "good" planning. By directly addressing the last key, structure and tools, this part provides a framework for obtaining management commitment and involvement. There is no guarantee on innovative ideas; creativity is not dependent on the methodology.

Chapter 1 redefines the classifical definition of planning. A new term, *Enterprise Analysis* (EA), a process separate from strategic, tactical, and operational planning, defines the process of linking business plans and MIS plans. Next, the characteristics of strategic systems are presented with examples. Then two of our planning methodologies (Technology Scan, Architecture Planning) are introduced and compared with other popular techniques of defining business needs: IBM's Business System Planning (BSP), Critical Success Factors (CSF), strategic alignment, Business Process Redesign, and the Cambridge Process.

Chapter 2 provides detail on the Technology Scan, an eight-step process providing insight into how technology is used in a company. This "reverse or backward" technique starts with what exists rather than what is needed. By analyzing ratios of knowledge workers to different forms of technology, voids are easily identified. This process can considerably enhance Business System Planning.

The scan data in Chapter 2 (Fig. 2.3) changes significantly

over time. End-user computing now rivals host computing in overall corporate expense. Also, the new RISC computers provide an astonishing breakthrough on MIPS (million instructions per second) pricing. The $80,000–100,000 per MIPs mainframe costs is competing with $800 per MIPS RISC computers. Software for LAN and client servers is also significantly less than on the mainframe. Future technology scans are assured to provide different cost ratios.

Chapter 3 explains the tools of architecture planning: architecture charts, planning matrix, and project worksheet. Also, a comparison to IBM's BSP is included.

A methodology should complement an organization's environment and management style. A combination of methods is likely. Also, if a corporation is struggling with the process, established consulting firms have specialists to assist.

CHAPTER 1

*Enterprise Analysis**

Over a number of years, an MIS planning system has evolved. When the effort started back in 1977–78, the primary purpose was to forecast programmer staffing needs. Since then, the purpose of the plan has expanded as the process was enhanced. In 1979, we added DP internal communication to the plan; in 1980, corporate communication; in 1981–83, portfolio selection; in 1984, strategy selection; and in 1985, technology scan. The current process is both more sophisticated and beneficial to the corporation. It now consists of a three-step process entitled Enterprise Analysis or EA (see Figure 1.1). The objective is to achieve an optimal MIS portfolio by integrating business and MIS plans and selecting the appropriate technology for implementation.

Some major observations resulting from the evolution of EA are:

- The classical definition of planning is inadequate—combining the four types of planning (strategic, tactical, operational, and business) is too confusing.

*Adapted from Johnson, James R. "Enterprise Analysis." *Datamation* (Dec. 15, 1984), pp. 97–103.

FIGURE 1.1. Enterprise Analysis (EA).

Step 1 *Define Needs*	*Step 2* *Select a Strategy*	*Step 3* *Establish Budget and Implement*
Understand existing support	Traditional Life Cycle	Net Present Value
Link business objectives to MIS planning	Prototyping	Portfolio Analysis
Document plans consistently	Information Center	Corporate Needs
	Office Systems	System Voids
	Personal Computer	Strategic Emphasis
	CAD/CAM	

- Technology has changed the nature of MIS planning—consideration of personal computers, office automation, prototyping and information centers are requirements.
- Various planning methodologies exist that can be tailored to an individual company. It is important to select a technique that fits the corporate culture.

MIS planning will continue to be one of the most challenging tasks facing a corporation. Hopefully, our experiences will help others improve their planning methods.

A survey on MIS planning systems (called "Information Systems Planning to Meet Business Objectives—A Survey of Practices") conducted by the New York consulting company Cresap, McCormick and Paget, concluded the following:

> *Although companies employ a variety of techniques and approaches, success in planning is surprisingly unaffected by such factors as industry, size of enterprise, methodology used, and organizational arrangements.*
>
> *What does seem to make a difference is the enterprise's approach to business planning, and efforts to establish links between the processes for business planning and those for information systems planning.*
>
> *In summary, it appears that the will to achieve linkage between information systems and business objectives outweighs all other factors.*

The "will to achieve" is directly linked to the strategic impact of information systems in an individual company. In companies where systems provide a competitive advantage or contribute to bottom-line profit, the will to achieve will exist. But can the efforts to establish links between business and information plans be better defined, and, if so, what are the options and steps?

A few years ago, MIS planning consisted of ranking those systems development projects that were destined for the traditional project life cycle. More recently, new technology has altered dramatically the options for solving MIS problems. But before exploring EA, it is appropriate to redefine planning.

A planning process and its related documents have numerous definitions. For example, one company may define an MIS plan simply as the strategic, long-range policies of a division. Others may include a combination of the following: hardware conversion plans, portfolio selection, capacity plans, control strategies, organization plans, project implementation procedures, and budget preparation activities. Since MIS planning has so many possible meanings, it is important to establish a definitional framework.

Thus, a fourth planning process, EA, has been added to the classical definition of strategic, tactical, and operational planning. The function is not new; it has been part of MIS strategic and tactical planning for years. Extracting the activity from the other three planning processes provides a corporation with the opportunity to concentrate on a specific objective. Figure 14.2 outlines the issues and parties responsible for the four planning processes. The arrows point out the relationship tactical business planning has to EA and, subsequently, the impact EA has on strategic and tactical MIS planning.

STRATEGIC PLANNING PARAMOUNT

Strategic planning is the highest level of MIS planning and ideally should involve the steering committee and/or senior management. The primary concerns are decentralizing (dispersion of MIS staff), integrating the islands of technology (MIS, office automation, communications), providing MIS infrastructure (data and application architecture), and controlling resources (use of charge-back, measurement of performance, enforcement of standards), and selecting the EA methodology.

With direction established in these strategic areas, MIS is in a position to perform divisional or tactical planning. If the direc-

FIGURE 1.2. Classical definition of planning, revised.

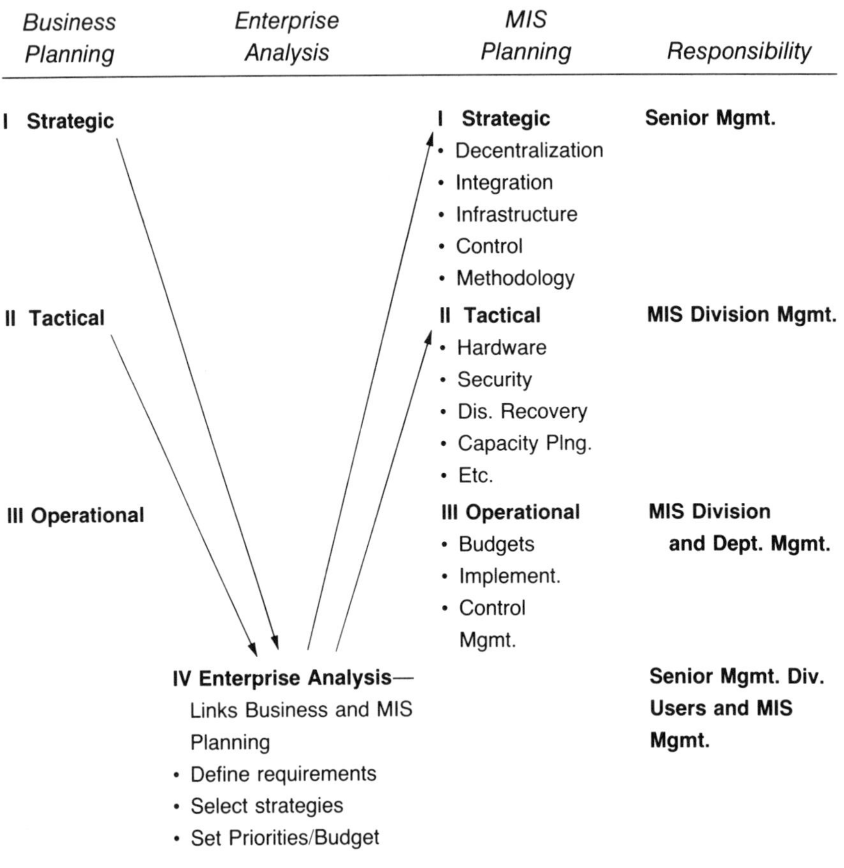

Business Planning	*Enterprise Analysis*	*MIS Planning*	*Responsibility*
I Strategic		**I Strategic** • Decentralization • Integration • Infrastructure • Control • Methodology	**Senior Mgmt.**
II Tactical		**II Tactical** • Hardware • Security • Dis. Recovery • Capacity Plng. • Etc.	**MIS Division Mgmt.**
III Operational		**III Operational** • Budgets • Implement. • Control Mgmt.	**MIS Division and Dept. Mgmt.**
	IV Enterprise Analysis— Links Business and MIS Planning • Define requirements • Select strategies • Set Priorities/Budget		**Senior Mgmt. Div. Users and MIS Mgmt.**

tion is not clearly defined by senior management, then the responsibility for setting direction on these issues falls to MIS management. In either case, the strategic planning must precede the tactical planning. A tactical MIS plan addresses the critical issues for a six- to 18-month horizon, such as: CASE Strategy, Hardware migration, Disaster recovery, Software migration, Change control, Training, Project management, Capacity planning, Security, and Service-level agreements

Finally, operational MIS planning is composed of three parts: budget preparation, design and implementation, and control management.

Having positioned EA with the classical types of planning, it is now appropriate to discuss in detail each of the three EA steps: defining needs, selecting strategies, and setting priorities/budgets.

Defining needs. To help accomplish this step, there are seven methodologies: IBM's Business System Planning (BSP), Critical Success Factors (CSF), Strategic Alignment, Business Process Redesign, Cambridge Process, Architecture Planning, and Technology Scan.

Each methodology has unique techniques to understand existing MIS support, link business objectives and MIS planning, and document results.

The seven methodologies address the same overall objective of defining needs, but each has certain strengths that may be complementary in some situations. Basically, the thrust of each is as follows:

- BSP—A one-time, analytical method that allows trade-off decisions producing a balance of short- and long-term projects. BSP planning starts by defining the ideal system.
- Critical Success Factors—Starts with top management critical needs and then defines measures necessary to satisfy these needs. This general approach may also apply to business planning and/or MIS planning.
- Strategic Alignment—Identifies the organization's objectives, pressure points, gray cells, and action plan.
- Business Process Redesign—After defining existing conditions, the desired future state is documented. Cross-divisional task forces are established to define opportunities in a condensed time frame (2–4 months).
- Cambridge Process—The most expeditious means of identifying strategic needs. After a CSF study, a prototype system is built in weeks with open architecture technology. The prototype may access real data bases, both internal and external to the corporation.
- Technology Scan—An eight-step process analyzing how technology is employed by knowledge workers (see Chapter 2).
- Architecture planning—A continuous planning process that forces visibility and administers the planning process. It starts by defining existing support and then links corporate direction to MIS support via the planning matrix (see Chapter 3).

By merging tools from different methods, a company may tailor its approach allowing for differences in culture, size, and organization structure.

Selecting a Strategy. Step one of EA defines what the corporate needs are, and step two addresses how to satisfy these needs. Our portfolio of strategies is shown in Figure 1.3. The basic breakdown is internal MIS development, outside resources, and end-user computing. Within each category three to four subcategories exist, bringing the total number of strategies to 12. Most corporations would have similar options available, although variations exist depending on the status of technology integration. As stated earlier, technologies like prototyping, information centers, decision support, office systems, and the personal computer have created additional options for addressing MIS problems.

The most recent option, cooperative processing, is a form of distributed processing. It involves using a PC for some processing (typically the user interface), possibly a LAN (server) and usually a host. The term client/server is used synonymously but could be considered a sub-set of cooperative processing.

Software is Unix based with options, such as ORACLE relational data base and C or C+, an object oriented language where data is surrounded by code that mediates access to the data.

FIVE PLANNING METHODOLOGIES

Business Systems Planning (BSP) The BSP method has been offered as a market support program by IBM since 1970. It was developed as a result of internal IBM experiences during the late 1960s.

In 1975, a cookbook-type manual was published that explained the procedure and tools of BSP. The document has been updated since then. The most recent version (1987) is about 100 pages, including appendixes, and provides excellent instruction on the technique.

In BSP, a project team chaired by a user-manager analyzes information needs from the top down to create a data plan for building information systems from the bottom up. The study is

FIGURE 1.3. Strategies for satisfying information needs.

A. Internal MIS Development	*B. Purchasing Outside Resources*	*C. End-User Computing*
Traditional Life Cycle • Initial Investigation • Feasibility Study/ General Design • Detail Design • Implementation	*Contract Programming* • Special Skills • Supplement Corporate Staff • One-Time Requirements	*Ad Hoc Retrieval/ Decision Support* • Batch Reporting • On-line Retrieval • Simulation/ Modeling • Data Analysis • Graphics
Prototyping • Develop system without life-cycle approach Similar to Research & Development	*Timesharing Network* • Special Software Tools • Immediate Access • Variety of Packages	*Independent Systems* • Data Entry • Department Subsystems • Production Jobs
Purchased Appl. Software • Follows Traditional Life Cycle but detail design and programming are minimized	*Turnkey Systems* • Integrated Hardware and Software Package for Specific Purpose	*Personal Computing* • Spreadsheets • Communications • Applications • Files/List • Processing • Word Processing • Graphics
Information Center • Write ad hoc requests • Consult • Develop Small Systems		*Office Systems* • Word Processors • Clustered Systems • Electronic Mail • Teleconferencing
		Cooperative Processing • Client/Servers

FIGURE 1.3. Continued

A. Internal MIS Development	*B. Purchasing Outside Resources*	*C. End-User Computing*
		• RISC Computers • LAN • Unix

generally a one-time effort and concentrates on ideal information needs. The two basic tools supporting the planning are the process-to-data matrix and process-to-organization matrix. The analyses do not result in design specifications or complete cost-benefit determinations. To get to that level of detail, additional analysis must be performed.

Critical Success Factors (CSF) The primary purpose of the CSF methodology, which was documented by John F. Rockart in the March-April 1979 *Harvard Business Review* article, "Chief Executives Define Their Own Data Needs," is to identify the "information needs of the chief executive officer or any other top executive of the company."

CSF consists of the following steps:

- Interviewing top management and discussing goals
- Analyzing goals and determining CSFs (three to six in number)
- Defining the prime measures of the CSFs
- For hard information, defining report formats and/or subsystems
- For soft information, recording appropriate data manually

CSFs can be arrayed hierarchically and used as an important vehicle by management for communication, either as an informal planning aid or as part of the formal planning process. CSF is an excellent approach for executives to clarify priorities both for business planning and MIS requirements.

Strategic Alignment Strategic alignment methodology has been documented over the years (1986–1988) in the bimonthly publication *Stage By Stage*. A variety of topics in addition to Strategic Alignment are covered, such as: transformation (downsizing and restructuring), political tactics, executive awareness, network organization, economics of computing, information utility, productivity, etc. However, the specific technique paralleling Enterprise Analysis is titled Strategic Alignment. It consists of four steps.

- Identify organization objectives:

  Productivity Improvement—investments that increase the output per unit of labor input (resulting in lower costs, higher ROI).

  Competitive Advantage—investments to create new products, features, or customer benefits (resulting in marketplace advantage, product differentiation).

  Management Effectiveness—investments to improve management's effectiveness (e.g., enhance communication, improve decision quality).

- Identify the pressure points:

  Priority Job Families—which job families (e.g., engineers, accountants, secretaries) have the greatest impact on your business objectives?

  Priority Processes—which processes (e.g., design, materials flow, cash flow) have the greatest impact on your business objectives?

  Priority Functions—which business functions (e.g., finance, manufacturing, operations, marketing, etc.) have the greatest impact on your business objectives?

  Priority Products—which products (e.g., remote terminals, product databases) have the greatest impact on your business objectives?

- Identify the gray cells:

  What investments in technology will address the pressure points? The categories are: Corporate Systems, Professional Support Computing, and Physical Automation.

- Implementation plan:

  Lay out a time-phased plan to implement technology.

BUSINESS PROCESS REDISIGN—BPR (marketed by Index Technologies) The methodology is similar to strategic alignment but with totally different terminology. Rather than identify objectives, BPR states initiatives, for example, winning through information technology leadership. Rather than defining pressure points, BPR defines leverage points, for example, establishing a partnership between MIS and the divisional users. Rather than gray cells, BPR defines gaps. Both methodologies incorporate charts similar to those described in architecture planning (see Chapter 3).

The intent is to pursue breakthrough opportunities, radical new models of business process, that require a major business change. The Ford distribution example cited below illustrated this type of change. As with other methodologies, top management support and a cross divisional team is essential. Also consulting help is essential to execute the methodology.

THE CAMBRIDGE PROCESS (marketed by the Cambridge Technology Institute, Cambridge, MA.) Of the methodologies discussed, the Cambridge Process can be executed in the shortest time. By using a special technology in the life cycle process, the duration from identifying strategic applications to application modeling is eight weeks:

Week	*Activity*
One	The Hunt—identifying opportunity and business case, CSF used
Two	Scope—prioritize functionality
Three/Four	Design—concentrated user design of functions
Five/Eight	Application Modeling—prototype user transactions with real data

The Unix based prototyping technology "surrounds" existing applications (extracts data) and provides interface to PCs, Fax, voice response, imaging, external data bases, etc. In other words, cooperative processing is obtained with an open architecture, one independent of vendor.

The auto parts application discussed below was prototyped

with this technology in one day! The production system if installed with the same Unix technology also has a short elapsed time, approximately 20 weeks.

Technology Scan Technology Scan is an eight-step process providing insight on how a company employs technology. With knowledge workers per division as the base, a ratio for each technology is calculated and compared with the corporate average. Discrepancies may indicate areas of opportunity, opportunity for technology to improve the productivity of knowledge workers. The technique is considered a "backward" process since it starts with what exists rather than needs (see Chapter 2).

Architecture Planning The architecture planning methodology was explained by this author in the May 1986 issue of *Information Management Year Book.* Understanding how existing MIS systems support a company is accomplished by linking MIS systems to functional business areas in graphic, nontechnical architecture charts.

The charts document the existing or proposed system support for a functional area—they link business functions to existing and proposed MIS systems. The criteria for a completed chart is that it must be understood by business managers with no more than 15 to 20 minutes of explanation. Flexibility and creativity are the guidelines when producing architecture charts. Developing a good product is a trial and error evolutionary process.

Business objectives are linked to MIS planning via a planning matrix. The matrix lists user division/department/group on the vertical axis and the following appears on the horizontal axis:

- Planning environment—this is the direct link to the corporate plan
- Current support
- Work-in-progress
- Projected needs (one to three years)
- Projected needs (beyond three years)

The last four items should be linked to the architecture charts. A project worksheet documents projects and requirements defined during the process (see Chapter 3).

STRATEGIC SYSTEMS

Identifying strategic information systems, the new title for defining information needs, is currently a highly visible activity in the business world. Companies have utilized technology to achieve competitive advantage by providing better customer service and simplifying business processes.

But what is a strategic information system? A few companies famous for systems are American Airlines (SABRE), Otis Elevator, and American Hospital Supply (ASAP). General characteristics of strategic systems and less known examples follow:

CUSTOMER FOCUS—IMPROVED CUSTOMER SERVICE, BETTER CUSTOMER INFORMATION, LOWER CUSTOMER COSTS.

Auto parts store

- Customer needs one hub cap for older model car.
- Sales person accesses manufacturer's service catalog via terminal. The computer cross-references the part to an auto parts inventory (external data base) and provdes purchase price.
- Customer views hub cap on screen (imaging) to confirm proper type.
- Fax of image sent to warehouse to confirm correct hub cap. Delivery expected in two to 2–3 hours.
- Customer calls to check if delivered. Voice response unit says part is at store.
- When customer picks up the hub cap, transaction is processed on workstation (cooperative processing) and then entered into central computer which updates inventory, records sale, and lists other specials or product related purchases (expert system) and associated discounts to encourage additional sales.

PROCESS CHANGE—RE-DESIGNING THE BUSINESS PROCESS TO BE MORE FLEXIBLE AND TIMELY.

Ford

- Engineers made the parts warehousing system efficient but the process was not effective. Thus, a team of industrial engineers combined forces with MIS professionals to re-design the parts distribution process with the objective of improving a customer service, and reducing costs.
- The 18 warehouses were reduced to eight, bar coding eliminated data entry, and terminals eliminated paper. By placing the parts on a carousel like those at dry cleaners, workers did not have to walk to part storage locations.
- With the new system, rush orders were shipped on the same day. Also there were fewer stock-outs because each warehouse has larger inventories.
- The new system provided on-line status of all orders.

PREEMPTIVE—FIRST TO OFFER THE SERVICE.

Pizza

- Customer calls to order pizza. Voice response unit asks for phone number and, if repeat customer, asks if regular order is desired (since many people order same number and type of pizzas periodically). If so, computer confirms order and starts pizza.
- If not a repeat customer, voice response unit can take information via touch tone: Phone Number, Pizza Size, Number of Pizzas, Ingredients, and Crust Type.
- To facilitate ordering, the sequence of questions and possible responses is on the box of each pizza delivered.

CROSS-DIVISIONAL—SYNERGY PROVIDED BY UNIQUE USE OF INFORMATION OR COMBINING DATA FROM MULTIPLE AREAS.

Johnson Wax

- Cross-divisional team designs customer focused order processing system.

- Information related from multiple data bases: Order Entry, Invoicing, Credit Checking, Customer Service, Distribution, and Inventory.
- Electronic data interchange (EDI) provides communication among customer, warehouse, and carriers.
- New department established for customer service. Inventories reserved and schedules maintained.
- Sales reps use laptops to check order status.

How sustainable is a strategic system? Max Hopper (Senior VP of Information Systems at American Airlines) has recently made perceptive comments on sustainability (HBR, May–June, 1990):

> *Today, however, SABRE is neither a proprietary competitive weapon for American Airlines nor a general distribution system for the airline industry. It is an* electronic travel supermarket, *a computerized middleman linking suppliers of travel and related services (including Broadway shows, packaged tours, currency rates) to retailers like travel agents and directly to customers like corporate travel departments. It takes only 30 days for a travel agent who is unhappy with SABRE to pull the system out and install a competing system. If a reservation system can be replaced within a month by a rival system, can it really be considered a source of enduring competitive advantage? The old interpretations of SABRE simply no longer apply. While it is more dangerous than ever to ignore the power of information technology, it is more dangerous still to believe that on its own, an information system can provide an enduring business advantage. The old models no longer apply.*

His conclusion: companies must focus on building electronic platforms that can transform their organizational structures and support new ways of making decisions. Following this logic religiously changes the way most people think about strategic systems since a platform internal system is not directly customer focused.

COMPARING EXPENSES AND MEDIA

Before discussing other strategies, it is interesting to compare the breakdown from two perspectives: current budget expense (people and hardware); and attention received from TV, magazines, and any other medium. Acknowledging subjectivity in my estimated numbers, consider Figure 1.4. Note the complete reversal of the internal MIS development strategy and end-user computing strategy in the two columns defining percent of budget (55 percent and 40 percent to 40 percent and 55 percent). From a budget expense perspective, internal MIS development is still greater (55 percent), but if perceived importance relates to attention received, then the PC is the prominent strategy. It may be that over the next five years, the budget will migrate toward the attention-received percentages. In selecting a strategy, however, understanding the strategy and relationships among strategies is important. In the ensuing paragraphs, comments on two technology strategies are included: information centers, and PCs.

FIGURE 1.4. Strategy: Budget vs. perception.

Strategy	*Current % of Budget*	*% Attention Received*
Internal MIS Development		
Traditional Life Cycle	35	20
Prototyping	5	5
Purchased Software	5	5
Information Center	10	10
	55	40
Outside Resources		
Contract Programming		
Timesharing	5	5
Turnkey Systems		
	5	5
End-User Computing		
Decision Support	5	5
Independent Systems	5	0
Personal Computers	25	45
Office Systems	5	5
	40	55
Total	100	100

TWO TYPES OF ICs EVOLVE

Two types of information centers (IC) have evolved. The first type directly supports end-user computing by providing consulting expertise on user languages, databases, network procedures, and so forth. The end user does the work. In the second type of IC, the consulting services include programming ad hoc requests and implementing small systems (five to 50 man-days).

If user programming expertise varies considerably within corporate divisions, which is usually the case, the second approach may be warranted. The philosophy is to attack the MIS backlog by providing alternate service paths, depending on the size and type of request. Figure 1.5 illustrates the alternative paths. Each path has a unique priority scheme—the longer the lead time, the more sophisticated the service path.

PCs are a new and increasingly desirable way for users to satisfy their MIS needs. Spreadsheet analysis, graphics, minor applications, file/list processing, and communication are all functions that can be done on a host or PC.

Establishing a corporate PC learning center has become a popular approach to user training. Corporate and individual users have demonstrated an unprecedented eagerness to learn about computers. During this learning stage, tight control and justification procedures will inhibit development. Initially, a relative priority approach is more appropriate than a net present value (NPV) method. Also, encouraging selection of software packages instead of tailored programming is a sound philosophy.

FIGURE 1.5. Alternate service path.

Path	*User Wait Average Queue*
Traditional Life Cycle (TLC)	1–2+ years
Prototyping	6–18 months
Purchased Software	2–6 months
Small System Implementations (IC)	1–2 months
Ad Hoc Requests (IC)	1–2 days
Consulting for End-User Computing (IC)	1–2 hours

As a strategy, the use of PCs is not new. The concept is a revision of distributed processing or individual processing. Future system design must consider the capabilities and role of PCs; both inputs and outputs may be processed via PCs or the host computer. This option presents interesting challenges to designers.

What obstacles stand in the way of successfully integrating these concepts? First, there are psychological obstacles within MIS to some of the new technologies. Staffing an information center, or offering PC consulting services are ways of operation that necessitate change; resistance within MIS can be expected. But assuming the technologies are established as strategies, the choices are still difficult. When considering end-user computing versus MIS, multiple departments are involved, and politics may become an issue; also, the roles of the host and PC overlap for some functions.

Management approaches to resolve the last two difficulties include analyzing the company's current approaches, joint planning with MIS departments and user groups, and communication and discussion on the merits of these various strategies.

Setting Priorities/Budgeting. This is the final step of EA. Two common techniques for ranking projects are ranking by net present value (NPV) and portfolio analysis. Ranking projects by their NPV is an excellent technique when benefits are tangible —as is generally the case with operational systems. But for management control and strategic planning systems, intangible benefits become the primary justification and the determination of dollar values is always a problem. Thus, NPV is not an absolute resource allocation technique and may not provide acceptable rankings.

Assessing project risk and then developing a portfolio of projects based on risk profiles is the second popular technique. Risk in this context includes the reliability of project size estimates, the value of intangible benefits, an assessment of the technological problem and project structure.

Each of the EA methods also provides tools for setting the priorities of projects. BSP and CSF rank subsystems based on corporate need; Strategic Alignment uses pressure points and gray cells; Business Process Redesign utilizes leverage points; the

Cambridge Process exercises the hunt; Architecture Planning employs graphic charts and expenditure trends along with strategic emphasis programs; and Technology Scan links knowledge workers to different technologies.

The priority process is company dependent, and selection criteria may vary from year to year based on experiences and, certainly from a pragmatic aspect, budget dollars available (corporate profitability). Nevertheless, the tools mentioned above should significantly enhance the priority setting process.

By acknowledging EA, defining corporate requirements, identifying strategies that include the new technologies, and developing criteria for budget decisions, management has the best chance of making the right decisions.

REFERENCES

Allen, Brant. "An Unmanaged Computer System Can Stop You Dead." *Harvard Business Review* (Nov.–Dec. 1982), 77.

Burns, William J. and McFarlan, Warren F. "Information Technology Puts Power in Control Systems," Harvard Business Review (Sept. –Oct. 1987), 89.

Business Systems Planning—Information Systems Planning Guide, Application Manual, GE20-0527. IBM Corporation (April 1987).

Buss, Martin D. "How to Rank Computer Projects." *Harvard Business Review* (Jan.–Feb. 1983), 118.

Cash, J. I., and Konsywski, B. R. "IS Draws Competitive Boundaries." *Harvard Business Review*, (March–April 1985), 134.

Cole, Robert E. "Target Information for Competitive Performance." *Harvard Business Review*, (May–June 1985), 100.

Donovan, John J. *Crisis In Technology*, Cambridge Technology Group, Inc., Cambridge, MA, 1990.

Donovan, John J. "Beyond Chief Information Officer to Network Manager," Harvard Business Review (Sept.–Oct. 1988), 134.

Hammer, Michael. "Reengineering Work: Don't Automate, Obliterate," Harvard Business Review (July–August 1990), 104.

Hopper, Max D. "Rattling SABRE—New Ways to Compete on Information," Harvard Business Review (May–June 1990), 118.

McFarlan, Warren F. "Portfolio Approach to Information Systems." *Harvard Business Review* (Sept.–Oct. 1981), 142.

Norton, David P. "The Economics of Computing in the Advanced Stages" in *Stage by Stage*. Nolan, Norton, Lexington, Mass. (1986–1988).

Pantages, Angeline. "The New Order at Johnson Wax," Datamation (March 15, 1990), 130.

Porter, M. E., and Millar, V. E. "How Information Gives You Competitive Advantage." *Harvard Business Review,* (July–August 1985), 149.

Rockart, John F. "Chief Executives Define Their Own Data Needs." *Harvard Business Review* (March–April 1979), 81.

Stalk, George, Jr. "Time—The Next Source of Competitive Advantage," Harvard Business Review (July–Aug. 1988), 41.

Zachman, J. A. "Business Systems Planning and Business Information Control Study: A Comparison." *IBM Systems Journal, 21,* 1 (1982), 31–53.

CHAPTER 2

*Technology Scan**

A Technology Scan produces a snapshot of a corporation's technology resources. This snapshot may take the form of a matrix in which organizational entities are cross-referenced with types of technology. Its premise is that a corporation's MIS resources and needs may be better understood by comparing relative counts of "things" such as PCs, CRTs, and word processors, to the number of "knowledge workers," a subset of all employees.

We conducted a technology scan that required minimal effort—our data gathering took 200 hours and two elapsed months. The subsequent analysis, a comparison of ratios of various knowledge workers to available technology for major business divisions, has considerably enhanced our MIS strategic planning.

Companies seeking to scan and analyze their technology resources should follow eight basic steps.

The first step is to decide on the types of technology you're interested in. For us, these were MIS corporate systems, end-user computing on host mainframes, office automation, and departmental computers (see Figure 2.1).

*Adapted from Johnson, James R. "Taking a Technology Snapshot." *Datamation* (April 15, 1987) pp. 73–78.

FIGURE 2.1. Technology scan sample results.

Group Summary Chart for Hallmark

	Group I	*Group II*	*Group III*	*Group IV*	*Grand Total*
A. MIS Systems					
Support staff	34	28	49	5	116
Development staff	42	27	29	2	100
Programs on-line	265	304	865	15	1,449
Programs batch	1,843	1,818	3,218	183	7,062
CRTs	176	524	926	19	1,645
B. End-User Computing					
TSO sign-ons	140	75	397	14	626
On-line CPU S.L.A.*(hrs/mo)	14.5	9.5	8	4	36
Batch CPU S.L.A.*(hrs/mo)	30.5	17.5	13	3.5	64.5
C. Office Technology					
PC	79	54	44	23	200
Word processor	9	7	20	17	53
Clustered word proc.	9	0	2	1	12
D. Department Computers	3	9	6	1	19
Knowledge Workers	2,348	614	653	340	3,955

*Service-Level Agreement

We excluded some forms of technology that others may judge critical to their scan, such as programmable process controllers, numerically controlled machines, and other specialized machines in which a computer is purely an internal component. We decided to exclude physical automation equipment mainly because, in our company, the engineering department has responsibility in this area. This approach helped us keep the scan simple. Using similar logic, we eliminated CAD/CAM devices, because they are of specialized use and not managed by MIS.

The second step is to decide which items within each area to include—CRTs, PCs, etc. Keep in mind that all base data is in counts or numbers of items—no dollars are assigned at this time. Thus, complex calculations that consider the timing of purchase, equipment leases, software expenses, etc. are avoided. Later, average costs will be assigned when technology types are compared.

In our scan, the data recorded for host (mainframe) end-user computing consisted of the number of sign-ons, prime time CPU service-level agreements (hours per month) for on-line decision support activities, and batch CPU service-level agreements (hours per month).

Office technology covers many areas, e.g., PCs, word processing, business graphics, and other communication-related functions, such as facsimile. Our data included only the first two categories—PCs, standalone word processors (Displaywriter, IBM's discontinued model), and clustered word processors (IBM's 5520, also discontinued). The last type, departmental computers, was the least interesting. It was not possible to draw worthwhile conclusions from the amalgamation of equipment—19 computers and six different processors. However, in other corporations, collecting data on departmental computers might be a primary part of the scan, a central corporate issue.

The third step in the process is to complete a Technology Scan matrix for equivalent organizational levels. The result is analogous to a corporate balance sheet of technology. Organizational levels in our case were business groups and divisions.

Employees' potential for utilizing technology is the basis for comparing all scan data. Since not all employees have equivalent potential, the Technology Scan must also count knowledge workers—that is, employees who use, or have the potential to use, a form of computer technology to improve individual effectiveness. For our scan, the knowledge workers held four generic job titles: manager, professional, technician, and marketing representative. This definition did not consider manufacturing workers, office and clerical positions, or sales support. In numbers, the knowledge workers represented about 25 percent of the total employees (3,955 of 16,157).

RATIO VARIES BY INDUSTRY

The ratio of knowledge workers to the total employees obviously varies by industry. We identified knowledge workers with the help of our computerized personnel system, which classifies positions in generic job families. We requested a printout of the job families by group and division and then decided what positions to include as knowledge workers.

With the Technology Scan complete, ratio analysis—the fourth step in our process—can begin.

After experimenting with presentation approaches, we chose to compare relative percentages (see Figure 2.2, which is calculated directly from the data shown in Figure 2.1). In our scan, for example, we found that Group I has 59 percent of the knowledge

FIGURE 2.2. Group-level ratio analysis.

(Percent of Corporate-Wide Totals)	*Group I*	*Group II*	*Group III*	*Group IV*
A. MIS Ratios				
Support staff	29	24	42	4
Development staff	42	27	29	2
Programs on-line	18	21	60	1
Programs batch	26	26	46	3
CRTs	11	32	56	1
B. End-User Computing Ratios				
TSO sign-ons	22	12	63	2
On-line CPU S.L.A.*(hrs/mo)	41	27	23	9
Batch CPU S.L.A.*(hrs/mo)	47	27	20	5
C. Office Technology Ratios				
PC	37	26	21	16
Word processor	17	13	38	32
Clustered word proc.	75	0	17	8
D. Department Computers Ratios				
Computers	16	47	32	5
Knowledge Workers	59	16	17	9

*Service-Level Agreement

workers; we would therefore expect its percentage share of all technology resources to be close to 59 percent.

It wasn't. Such discrepancies must have an explanation; the fifth step in our process is to investigate them.

By itself, ratio analysis does not provide answers; it only identifies potential problems or opportunities. Ratios are mechanical tools, not intended as arbitrary standards of performance or a substitute for judgment. Deviations from "normal" indicate a different mode of operation, not necessarily a less effective operation. It's important to note that no industry guidelines for ratio analysis have been developed. In practice, with any type of ratio analysis, one question often leads to another and the search for a thorough understanding may take a significant amount of time.

To illustrate, consider how the CRT analysis breaks down in Figure 2.2. Group I, for example, with 59 percent of the total knowledge workers, has only 11 percent of the CRTs in our scan. Groups II and III, which together represent 33 percent of the total knowledge workers, account for 88 percent of the CRTs.

Why such a disparity? A look at business functions provides partial explanation. In our case, Group I (with less CRTs than expected) contains such relatively light users as the field-marketing organization and the "creative" division (including the staff artists). Groups II and III (more CRTs than expected) include divisions heavily dependent on corporate systems: manufacturing, finance, and distribution.

Certain "distortions" based on organizational idiosyncracies also must be considered in the analysis. For example, assuming CRTs are heavily used in the MIS division, the group including the MIS division will reflect the better numbers.

How valuable is this high-level analysis? Primarily by explaining the imbalances, it forces an understanding of business functions and implementation of technology. Unfortunately, what is right, the most effective allocation, is still subjective interpretation. In our ratio analysis at the relatively high (group) level, the most important observation was that, with the exception of clustered word processors, Group I had less than average utilization in all areas. Pursuing a full explanation required ratio analysis at a more detailed level.

We obtained more detail by analyzing ratios of division-level data (in our organization, division VPs report to group VPs). Analysis of some divisions produced no action items but rather provided confirmation that technology was being applied at a level we regarded appropriate. In other cases, however, division-level analysis led to many specific recommendations. For example, one division—Division C—that we considered critical to one of our primary corporate objectives, controlling nonproduct costs, was found to be underutilizing technology.

The most pertinent ratio in our analysis of Division C was the percentage of CRTs and on-line systems (7 percent) compared with the percentage of knowledge workers (21 percent). After the initial numbers were understood, a major effort was initiated to identify and better understand the opportunities in this division. A series of meetings was held with middle managers and an analyst was assigned for follow-up interviews, all with the objective of defining an aggressive five-year plan to make Division C competitive with other major divisions.

The sixth step in our process is to link scan results to existing MIS planning activities, proposing additional support for appropriate technology areas.

PROPOSING THE TYPES OF TECHNOLOGY

The most difficult aspect of the analysis is that of proposing the types of technology that will improve the effectiveness of a given organization. In our analysis of Division C, placing production databases on-line, increasing resources for end-user computing, and installing other enhancements to simplify the manual processing resulted as immediate action items.

The seventh step—recommended only for the advanced practitioner—is to calculate costs and make relative dollar comparisons of technology.

Having reviewed the raw data and the ratio analysis as expressed in percentages, we followed up by converting our results into dollars. To avoid complexity, average yearly depreciation costs were developed for the hardware; in our calculations, a CRT cost $350 per year, a PC $1,080 per year, and a CPU was charged out at $900 per hour.

The relative costs of the four forms of technology analyzed

are shown in Figure 2.3: MIS division, end-user computing, office technology, and departmental computers. It was somewhat surprising that end-user computing and office technology were only 4.5 percent and 2.7 percent, respectively, of the total spent per year. Almost 90 percent of all expenses were associated with major corporate systems. This may not be typical for the majority of companies, but we are highly centralized and the comparison places end-user computing and office technology in perspective based solely on dollars. For example, if we double the number of PCs, the direct out of pocket expense to the corporation goes up less than 1 percent. Some inconsistencies exist in the number because staff is included in the MIS system category but excluded in the other technology areas. Another interesting observation: $10.8 million is used to develop and support systems, which, on the average, generated another $3.5 million in hardware expense every year (reflecting a 35 percent annual growth).

The remaining step, the eighth, is to compare trends in subsequent years. Relative costs comparisons provide insight over static comparisons. Figure 2.4 shows the increases we found over a 12-month period. The $200,000 required for the four additional people to work on MIS projects is 40 percent of the approximately $500,000 spent in this 12-month period. It exceeds what was spent on adding the 236 CRTs ($82,600) and the 106 PCs ($114,480) combined. As a secondary benefit, this analysis provided after-the-fact visibility to the number of CRTs and PCs added.

Although significant value was derived from this eight-step process, the methodology discussed has a number of limitations. Some of the obvious data item limitations follow:

- The description of the knowledge worker was at a macro level, causing some inconsistencies. Since many of the CRTs and a large number of the production systems were not utilized by knowledge workers (per our definition), the analysis had to explain the discrepancies.
- Decentralized programming personnel not part of the MIS staff must be included if they are significant. In our case, they represented a small fraction of the total and were excluded.
- There is a hidden cost beyond hardware for both CRTs and personal computers: control units, installation, training, consulting, etc.

FIGURE 2.3. Scan results in dollars.

Type of Technology	Number Times Cost ($)		Total ($)	%
A. MIS Division				
Support	116 × 50,000		5,800,000	
Development	100 × 50,000		5,000,000	
Batch production				
On-line production			9,797,612	
CRTs	1,645 × 350		575,750	
	Subtotal	=	21,173,362	88.7
B. End-User Computing				
On-line CPU TSO	35/mo. × 12 × 900/hr.		378,000	
Batch CPU	64.5/mo. × 12 × 900/hr.		696,600	
	Subtotal	=	1,074,600	4.5
C. Office Technology				
PC	211 × 1,080		227,880	
Word processor	53 × 2,800		148,400	
Clustered word proc.	12 × 23,000		276,000	
	Subtotal	=	652,280	2.7
D. Department Computers	19 × 51,605*		980,495	
	Subtotal	=	980,495	4.1
	Grand Total	=	23,880,737	100.0

*Equipment costs are depreciation: purchase price divided by 5.
Also, department computer is average for 19 machines.

FIGURE 2.4. Trends.

Twelve Month Changes

	Group I	*Group II*	*Group III*	*Group IV*	*Totals*	*Dollars*[A]
1. S/D Support Staff	0	−4	+4	0	0	0
2. S/D Project Staff	+1	+3	0	0	+4	$200,000
3. CRTs	+39	+96	+92	+9	+236	$ 82,600
4. PCs	+43	+23	+19	+21	+106	$114,480
5. Word Processors	−2	+1	−2	+6	+3	$ 8,400
6. Clustered WP	+4	0	0	0	+4	$ 92,000
					Total	$497,480

[A]For equipment, depreciation

- The distinction between PCs as management tools and PCs as word processors was not noted. Clarification adds to the value of the office automation ratios.

The Technology Scan method might be criticized as a backward approach to defining corporate opportunities: rather than starting with information needs and working forward to system requirements, the methodology snapshots the existing corporation. This is a valid criticism because the scan is a reverse process; this "weakness," however, is also a strength, since all divisions receive an unbiased assessment.

THE EIGHT STEPS OF SCAN AND ANALYSIS

Step 1: Decide on technological "types" of interest.

Step 2: Decide on which "things" within each area to include: CRTs, personal computers, etc.

Step 3: Complete a Technology Scan matrix for equivalent organizational levels.

Step 4: Using relative percentages, compare the number of knowledge workers to areas of technology.

Step 5: When imbalances cannot be explained (based on function, future projects, etc.), do more detective work.

Step 6: Link results to existing MIS planning activities, proposing additional support for appropriate technology areas.

Step 7: For the advanced practitioner, costs may be included for relative dollar comparisons of technology.

Step 8: In subsequent years, compare trends.

CHAPTER 3

*Architecture Planning**

The comments of senior executives about their companies' management information systems (MIS) show weaknesses in traditional planning. Examples are:

- Why can't my business managers integrate their knowledge of corporate direction into the MIS requirements?
- What we need is a straightforward methodology that integrates corporate direction with MIS planning. The technique should be easy to understand and provide tools all divisions can use.

These comments reflect the inherent difficulty of linking MIS planning and corporate direction, a function defined as "enterprise analysis" and composed of three phases: defining needs, selecting strategies, and setting priorities. The popular methods used by many corporations to address the first phase are: IBM's BSP, Critical Success Factors, Strategic Alignment, and Technology Scan. This article documents another method which evolved

*Adapted from Johnson, James R. "Information Architecture." *Information Management Yearbook*. British Institute of Data Processing Management (1986), pp. 80–84.

over three-years. It is called Architecture Planning (AP), a term derived by combining the first word of the two primary tools (discussed later): *architecture* charts and *planning* matrix.

To define corporate needs, AP integrates three steps:

- Understanding MIS support
- Linking business objectives to MIS planning
- Documenting plans consistently

Figure 3.1 identifies the tools provided for each step and the responsible parties. Briefly, architecture charts define the existing and potential MIS support for each corporate division. The MIS group is in the best position to initially develop these charts. The conduit for linking business plans to MIS plans is called the planning matrix. It is primarily the responsibility of user division management. Consistent documentation is the purpose of the project worksheet, prepared by MIS and user management.

The cost or effort to perform AP was minimal. For the first three years, line DP management worked on the methodology. For the next two years, one full-time individual was assigned to

FIGURE 3.1. Architecture planning.

Step	*Tool*	*Responsible Parties (Primary/ Secondary)*
1 Understanding MIS support	Architecture charts a) present b) future	MIS
2 Linking business objectives to MIS planning	Planning matrix	Division managers/ MIS
3 Documenting plans consistently	Project worksheet and resulting graphics	MIS/division managers

aid in the process; however, after the methodology was established, the execution resided with line management.

Documenting the methodology, the three steps are explained sequentially.

STEP 1—UNDERSTANDING MIS SUPPORT

The first AP task is to document in graphic, nontechnical form the DP support for a functional business area. The methodology of AP proposes architecture charts as the appropriate tool.

Using business terms, architecture charts document the existing or proposed system support for a functional area. The criteria for a completed chart is that it must be understood by business managers with no more than 15 to 20 minutes of explanation. There are three techniques available: graphic, function, and flow. (See "Charting Techniques" below for examples of each.) The graphic approach depicts relationships among groups, relative magnitudes, interfaces and/or a hierarchical structure. The function chart links business functions to MIS systems in a logical manner. The flow graphics are more difficult to develop since they may illustrate sequence of events, processes, systems, organizations, and logical relationships. Flexibility and creativity are the guidelines when producing architecture charts. Developing a good product is a process of trial and error. If it requires more than 15 to 20 minutes to explain, the technique selected is wrong or more innovation is required.

The architecture charts developed, documented, and used in our company are as follows:

- *Graphic*
  resource allocation
  office automation
  information center
  project control
  international
- *Function*
  employee information
  finance
  manufacturing

- *Flow*
  marketing system
  marketing communication
  order processing

In meetings between MIS personnel and user division management, the architecture charts are used to provide a common understanding of the MIS support to each division.

STEP 2—LINKING BUSINESS OBJECTIVES TO MIS PLANNING

In AP step 2, the planning matrix is the tool used by divisional users to link business objectives to MIS planning. Figure 3.2 illustrates the matrix format. The first column defines the system user within a division. The planning environment (column 2) is the direct link with the corporate plan. If a division's business processes impact MIS, it is documented in this column. For example, if corporate personnel has a business objective with increased emphasis on security, it may have implications on the MIS systems.

The current system column reflects, in summary level, the detail of the architecture charts. Descriptive comments on batch versus on-line, and centralization versus decentralization are appropriate. The in-progress section defines existing projects or major enhancements. The information in Figure 3.2 was extracted from a real-life planning matrix completed by the employee information group. MIS had provided a starter document, but the end product was clearly superior to the MIS version. There were 10 user areas (corporate, compensation, payroll, benefits, organizational development, employment, employee relations, corporate training, fleet, and security) defined on the matrix. For simplicity, only the corporate users were selected to demonstrate the process.

To illustrate the technique, note the "planning environment" line, which notes a requirement for quick access to management information. As shown under the column "current system," MARK IV and SAS (both user programming languages) are currently in place. The next column (in-process) shows nothing in progress to address the issue; however, in column 5 (projected needs), the requirement is noted and a project is expected.

The final task for step 2 requires completion of the fifth and sixth columns on the planning matrix: projected needs for up to and beyond three years. The process is generally a group planning meeting among managers in the appropriate division. MIS personnel would not normally attend these sessions. Rather, MIS conducts initial meetings to explain the methodology and also develops an "initial" planning matrix for the division managers. Obviously, the responsibility for the planning must reside with divisional management. As part of this process, weaknesses are analyzed and opportunities defined.

To continue the employee information example, one of the projected needs in the one to three year time frame is to acquire a more user-friendly inquiry language. A related need is listed in the column "projected needs over three years," i.e., continue to expand user friendly ad hoc reporting capabilities. Another need in the one- to three-year period is to expand word processing and link it to the main computer system. If a division had a number of personal computers (PCs), a project linking them to various corporate databases would be appropriate. As demonstrated by this planning matrix, the divisional users have taken their planning seriously.

STEP 3—DOCUMENTING PLANS CONSISTENTLY

Within the hierarchy of documentation, the briefest form is the one-line description contained in the planning document. The next level of detail requires a project worksheet. The format of the worksheet and guidelines for completion are shown in Figure 3.3. The next level in the hierarchy would be a requirements/general design/feasibility study. A project worksheet is completed for all projects including those in the study, design, or implementation phase. This is done for two reasons. Firstly, to be sure that a common understanding exists on the description and justification. Secondly, because all projects may be subject to budget approval each year.

From the information on the worksheet, various summary documents can be produced, covering such themes as strategic

FIGURE 3.2. Employee information systems planning matrix.

1 System User	*2 Planning Environment*	*3 Current Systems*	*4 In-Process*	*5 Projected Needs (1–3 Years)*	*6 Projected Needs (Over 3 Years)*
Corporate	Increased emphasis on security Centralize and standardize information processing Quick access to increased amount of	Batch-oriented systems Paper and microfiche reports MARK IV, SAS for user information retrieval	Master file expansion	Enhance current system on-line inquiry on-line update Continue to centralize and standardize information processing for new and	Electronic mail testing Additional modelling and forecasting capabilities User "at-home" access to system Alternative

management information	existing locations and corporations Expand graphics capabilities Expand word processing and link to main computer data Acquire more user-friendly inquiry language Additional security	methods of data input (OCR, voice, etc.) Continue to expand user friendly ad hoc reporting capabilities Provide on-line use of system to remote users

FIGURE 3.3. Completion guidelines for the project worksheet.

Completed by:
Date:

A Project name:
(Self-explanatory. Either support or project.)

B Requested by:
(Sponsor for project.)

C Category:
(tick one)
Support —(minimum level to keep system running and/or do specific enhancements.)
On-going —(development projects carried over from one year to the next.)
Increment—(new development task or specific increase for support. If requirement is for a study only, it should be noted.)

D Description:
(A short paragraph that explains the project in business terms.)

E Justification:
(Justification is the reason for doing the project. It can be tangible dollar savings or intangible reasons; such as increased sales or better control. Mention investment analysis if completed. Quantify benefits when possible.)

F Strategic area:
(Also mention the corporate strategic area that will most likely be affected. Examples of strategic areas are:

1. Maintain operations
2. Volume development
3. Dealer profitability
4. Operating efficiency
5. Managerial control
6. Product quality
7. Leadership
8. Subsidiary growth)

G Departmental:
(Which departments are affected by this project? It may include others beside those which requested it.)

FIGURE 3.3. Continued

H Resources required (Primary project group is ....)

	Project Total	*Total 1990–94*	*This Year*	*Man-Years 1990*	*1991*	*1992*	*1993*	*1994*
Project								
Support								
Other								

(Indicate the primary systems development project group and man-years [rounded] to complete project over next five years. If completed in the five-year time frame, the support level to maintain is also shown. List any other systems development resources that were not identified in the primary project group as secondary project groups.)

I Equipment resources (CPU, CRT, Communications, etc.)
(Indicate projection of any specific computer equipment resources required. Examples are CRTs, printers, CPU resource, disk, communications needs, etc.).

areas impacted, equipment resources required, and staffing trends. By graphing this data by support, projects, and division, management can now reflect on the long-range impact of approved projects. It should be noted that the support requirements are continuing with a ratio of 5–10 man-years of development to one man-year of support. On rewrite projects, of course, support may also decrease or remain unchanged.

Item F, strategic areas, deserves separate comments. Contrary to popular opinion, strategic goals do not necessarily help with decision making. They are so general that virtually all activities fall within their scope. For example, cost cutting measures are strategic since they improve financial performance and operational efficiency. Modifying systems to simplify customer ordering is responding to customer needs, even though it might be labeled maintenance, an activity not generally considered strategic.

During this step, the long-range implications of system integration and database planning must also be considered. However, the business needs are primary, and technical considerations secondary.

COMPARING BSP TO AP

As mentioned in Chapter 1, other methodologies address phase one of enterprise analysis. After briefly discussing IBM's BSP, it will be compared with AP.

In BSP, information needs are analyzed from the top down to create a data plan for building information systems from the bottom up (designing the systems, however, is an implementation planning process and not part of BSP). In AP, systems are suggested, but the definition of data classes is not considered since it is a lower level of detail. Figure 3.4 shows the scope of AP.

SUPPORTING MATRIX

The two basic tools supporting the planning are the process-to-data matrix and process-to-organization matrix. BSP supports

FIGURE 3.4. The scope of AP.

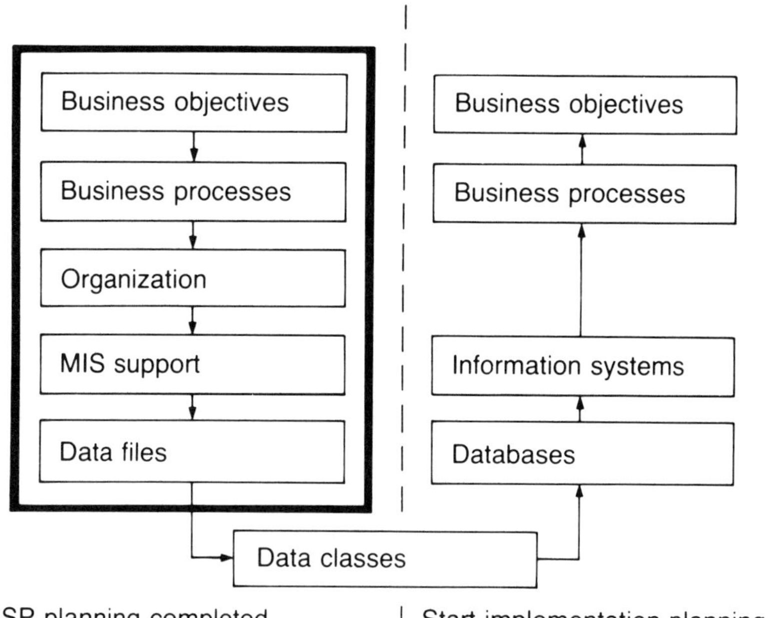

strategic decisions. The analysis does not result in design specifications or complete cost-benefit determinations. In order to get to that level of detail, additional analysis must be performed over and above the BSP study.

Both methodologies address the overall objectives of selecting the optimal portfolio of projects; but they each have their strengths and may be complementary in some situations. Figure 3.5 provides an overview of the two approaches and the tools applicable at each of the four steps. Additional comparative characteristics are:

- BSP is a one-time effort, usually six to eight weeks, while AP is a continuous planning process integrated with the budget process.
- Extensive training and support is available from IBM on the BSP method. Conversely, although it is a more intuitive process, this article is the only reference available for AP.
- Using the ideal system requirements (BSP) as opposed to the

FIGURE 3.5 Enterprise Analysis methodologies compared.

Business Planning Require-ments	*Architecture/Systems Planning*		*IBM's Business System Planning (BSP)*	
	Techniques and Tools	*Responsible Parties*	*Techniques and Tools*	*Responsible Parties*
1 Understand DP support	Architecture charts a) present b) future	MIS	Matrix charts: process/ organization; data class/ process	Sponsor and project team
2 Link business objectives to DP planning	Planning matrix	Division managers/MIS	Interviews; problem analysis sheet	Sponsor and project team
3 Document plans consistently	Project worksheet	MIS/Division managers	Information architecture; subsystem prerequisite; project report; funding scenario	Sponsor and project team

existing systems (AP) as a starting point shows a philosophical difference on how to initiate the process.

- The database concepts play a stronger role in BSP; application systems are the focus in AP.
- Both methodologies can be applied in either a centralized or decentralized corporation; no distinction exists on this point.

ANCILLARY BENEFITS

The primary benefit of AP is, of course, linking business and MIS planning in order to achieve an optimal MIS portfolio. A secondary benefit of MIS is credibility. For some MIS executives, this may be a priority. In our evolution, although improving credibility was definitely a factor, AP provided more of a conceptual framework for business systems and establishing common terminology. With regard to operating divisions, MIS becomes a facilitator of the planning process. From the MIS viewpoint, AP is a positive activity which improves internal communication.

Also, an architecture room containing supporting documentation and architecture charts is recommended as it provides a focal point for the entire program.

If your corporation does not have a methodology for defining needs, or if you are not satisfied with the process, consider AP as an alternative. The following steps are recommended:

- Select an individual to coordinate the effort.
- Start with the "opportunity" areas first, since it may take one or two years to implement throughout the entire corporation.
- Using the guidelines and examples illustrated in this chapter, define architecture charts and planning matrices for the selected areas.
- Review AP results with division managers in individual meetings. The top manager of the division should participate.
- After the divisions update the planning matrix, document the project worksheets.
- Analyze the database plan and system integration information to ensure that the short and long-term considerations are coordinated.

CHARTING TECHNIQUES

Three of the eleven basic Architecture Charts developed in our company are illustrated to explain the charting techniques: Graphic, Function, and Flow. The criteria for a completed chart is: business managers (nontechnical personnel) must comprehend the chart with no more than 15 to 20 minutes of explanation.

Examples of each technique will illustrate the concept.

- Graphic

  Figure 3.6 illustrates the Graphic technique, which is the simplest form of Architecture Chart. The three functions of the Information Center are listed in the center along with the software support available. The database interfaces are listed below the function box. The perimeter shows the business divisions that utilize the services. The Graphic technique may depict relationships among groups, relative magnitudes, interfaces, or hierarchical reporting.
- Function

  The Function chart lists business functions performed by a division or subdivision. It then graphically links the functions to business systems in a logical structure. For example, in the Financial architecture chart, Figure 3.7, the flow of the major financial functions is to the general ledger. There are also other support activities that do not directly interface with the general ledger. The MIS systems are listed below the double line in each box. The dots identify a separate MIS system or subsystem supporting the business function. For example, the function "record receivables" is supported by a Common Billing System. The function charts do not necessarily match directly back to the corporate organizational structure, since business functions are not always organizational entities.
- Flow

  Flow graphics involve integrated factors, such as sequence of events, processes, systems, organizations, and logical relationships. They are more difficult to develop but consequently may simplify a more complex situation.

  Figure 3.8 integrates a number of business functions but concentrates on the Marketing Support System. As in the prior nomenclature, the dots represent a system or subsystem. With this graphic, management can better understand the efforts devoted to account information and marketing reporting.

With each technique, a trial-and-error approach is recommended. Creativity and flexibility are the guidelines. These examples illustrate only existing support; long-range projects have also been developed in critical areas, such as electronic communication and retailer systems.

REFERENCES

Business Systems Planning—Information Systems Planning Guide. Application Manual GE20-0527. IBM Corporation (April, 1987).

FIGURE 3.6. Information center architecture.

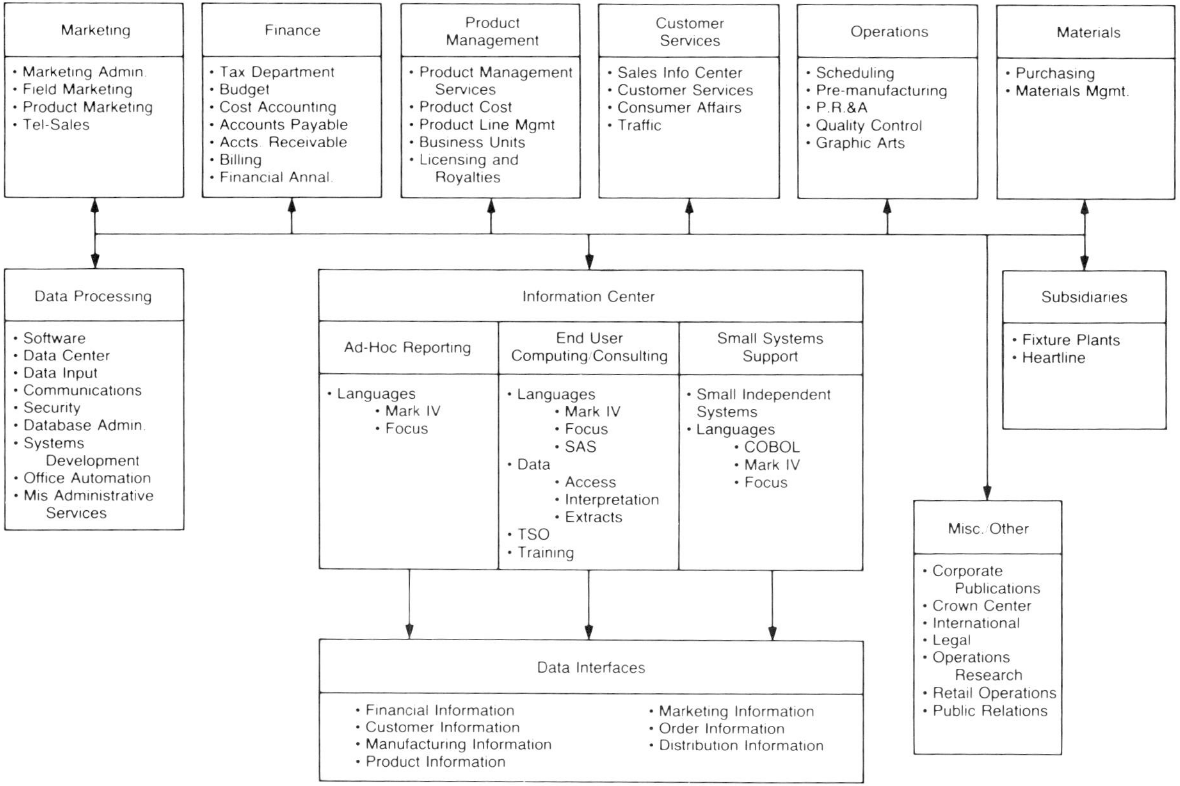

Marketing
- Marketing Admin.
- Field Marketing
- Product Marketing
- Tel-Sales

Finance
- Tax Department
- Budget
- Cost Accounting
- Accounts Payable
- Accts. Receivable
- Billing
- Financial Annal.

Product Management
- Product Management Services
- Product Cost
- Product Line Mgmt
- Business Units
- Licensing and Royalties

Customer Services
- Sales Info Center
- Customer Services
- Consumer Affairs
- Traffic

Operations
- Scheduling
- Pre-manufacturing
- P.R.&A
- Quality Control
- Graphic Arts

Materials
- Purchasing
- Materials Mgmt.

Data Processing
- Software
- Data Center
- Data Input
- Communications
- Security
- Database Admin.
- Systems Development
- Office Automation
- Mis Administrative Services

Information Center

Ad-Hoc Reporting
- Languages
  - Mark IV
  - Focus

End User Computing/Consulting
- Languages
  - Mark IV
  - Focus
  - SAS
- Data
  - Access
  - Interpretation
  - Extracts
- TSO
- Training

Small Systems Support
- Small Independent Systems
- Languages
  - COBOL
  - Mark IV
  - Focus

Subsidiaries
- Fixture Plants
- Heartline

Misc./Other
- Corporate Publications
- Crown Center
- International
- Legal
- Operations Research
- Retail Operations
- Public Relations

Data Interfaces
- Financial Information
- Customer Information
- Manufacturing Information
- Product Information
- Marketing Information
- Order Information
- Distribution Information

FIGURE 3.7. Financial systems architecture for corporate business functions.

Maintain Chart of Accounts	Record Receivables	Collect and Post Cash	Track and Depreciate Corporate Assets	Confirm Purchases, Reduce Liability	Compute Tax Liability, Cost of Goods Sold & Inv. Levels	Record Shipments	Report Business Expenses	Compute Non-Product Wages, Salaries, & Benefits	Accept Trial Balance Level Data From Subsidiaries
Automated Financial Reporting System	Common Billing System	Accounts Receivable System Automated Collection System Customer Claims Tracking System Royalty Income System Automated Lockbox System	Appropriations Accounting System Fixed Assets System	Accounts Payable System Royalties System	Finished Goods Inventory Cost System SAC Lifo / Fifo	Common Billing System	Business Expense System Long Distance Telephone Charge Back Wats Charge-Back	Employee Information System-Payroll and Benefits	Crown Center Redev. Corp. Domestic Retail Corp. Evensons Fixture Products Co. Hallmark International Hallmark Mkting Corp. Hallmark Retail Group Litho-Krome

Assets	Liabilities	Cost of Goods Sold	Other Non-Shipment Income	Departmental Expenses	Other Expenses	Equity

General Ledger (Includes Hallmark, Ambassador and Subsidiaries)

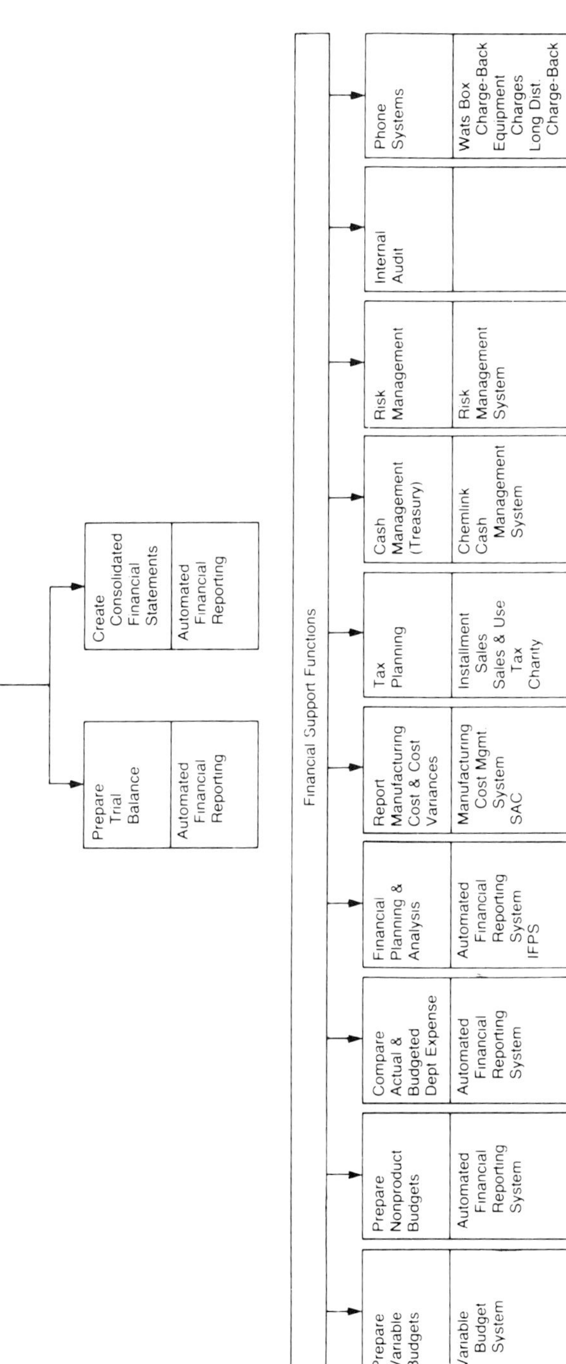

Prepare Trial Balance
Automated Financial Reporting
Create Consolidated Financial Statements
Automated Financial Reporting
Financial Support Functions
Prepare Variable Budgets
Variable Budget System
Prepare Nonproduct Budgets
Automated Financial Reporting System
Compare Actual & Budgeted Dept Expense
Automated Financial Reporting System
Financial Planning & Analysis
Automated Financial Reporting System IFPS
Report Manufacturing Cost & Cost Variances
Manufacturing Cost Mgmt. System SAC
Tax Planning
Installment Sales Sales & Use Tax Charity
Cash Management (Treasury)
Chemlink Cash Management System
Risk Management
Risk Management System
Internal Audit
Phone Systems
Wats Box Charge-Back Equipment Charges Long Dist. Charge-Back

FIGURE 3.8. Marketing system architecture for domestic social expression.

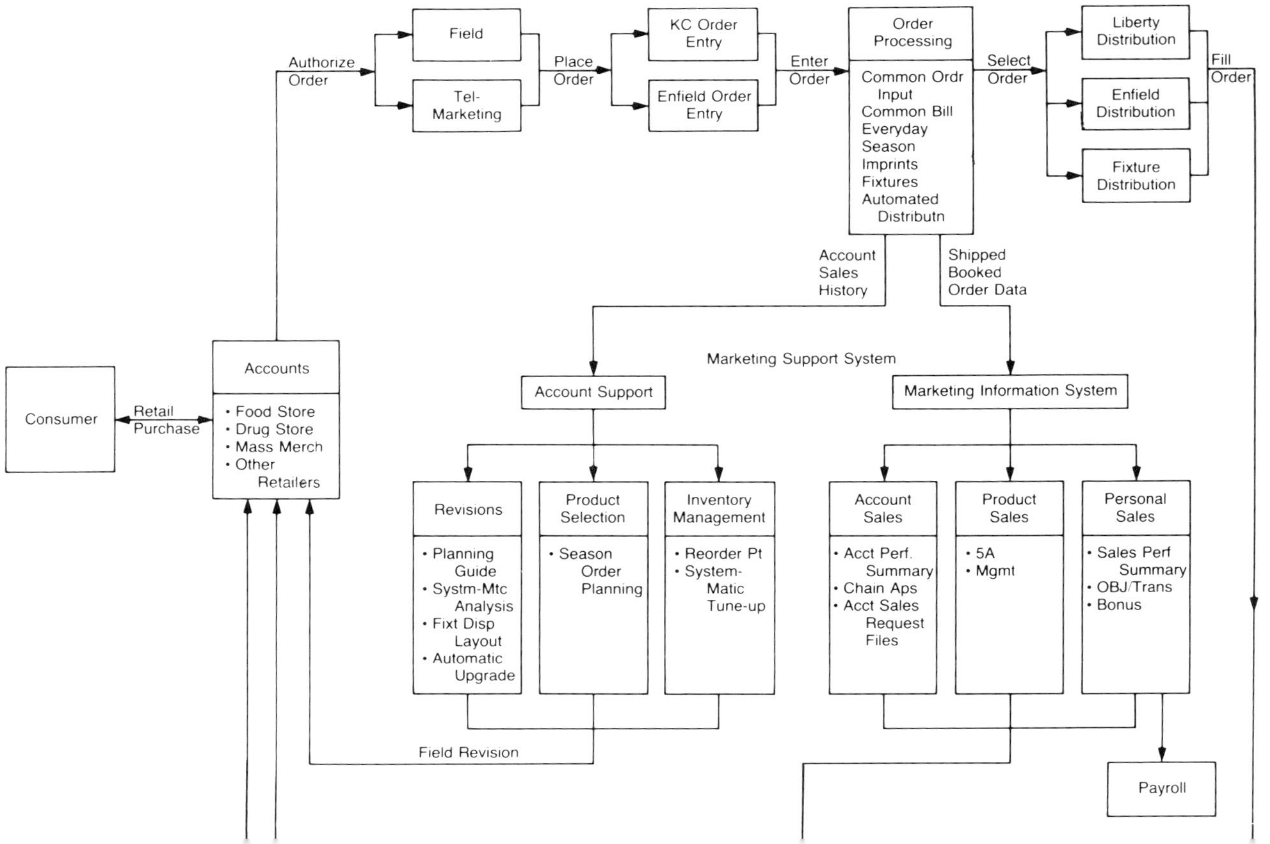

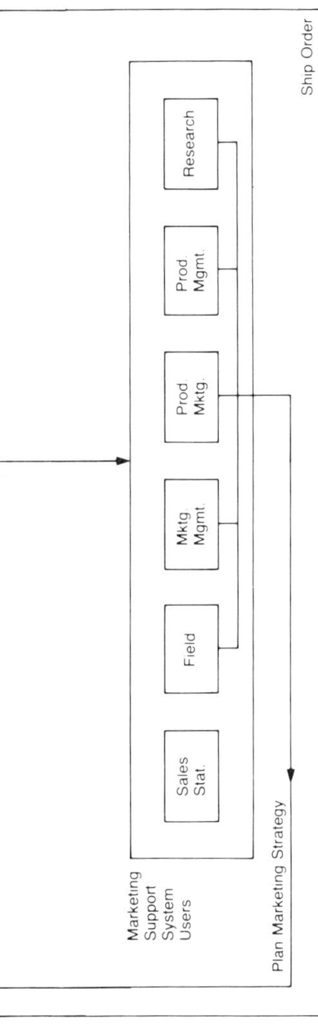

Ship Order
Research
Prod. Mgmt.
Prod. Mktg.
Mktg. Mgmt.
Field
Sales Stat.
Marketing Support System Users
Plan Marketing Strategy

PART II

Directional Tools

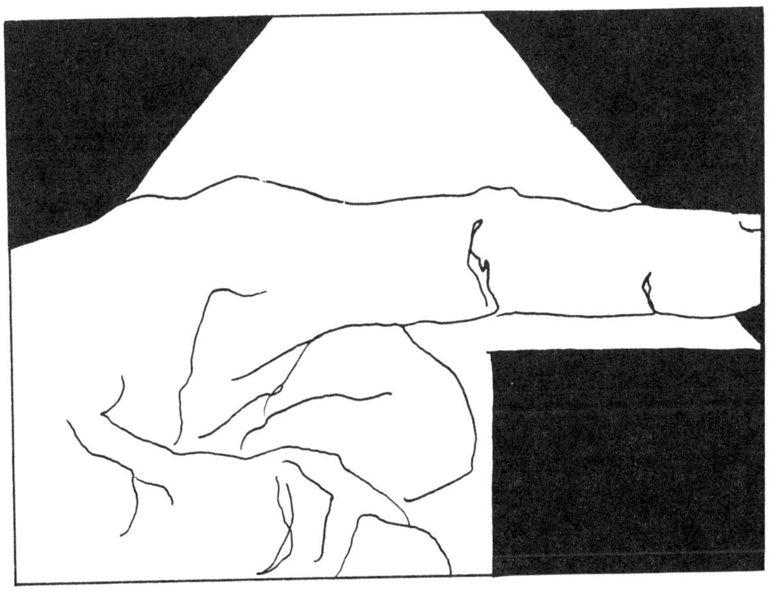

Each chapter in this second part addresses a major software development tool, tools with directional impact on the entire organization: CASE, Fourth-Generation Languages (4GLs), and Expert Systems (ES).

Computer Aided Software Engineering (CASE) tools, in the broadest sense, encompass any facility utilizing the computer to assist in the production of software. It is under this liberal definition that some vendors market code-restructuring tools and other products that indirectly impact the development process. A brief definition of CASE is:

Automating the systems development life cycle with tailored software.

CASE tools can be further subdivided: those that are directed primarily at the front-end activities of design and analysis and those that are focused on the implementation functions of code generation, testing, and maintenance. Recently, the terms *Upper* CASE and *Lower* CASE have been adopted to distinguish these products.

Chapter 4 (CASE Strategies) provides a non-traditional approach by introducing inherent barriers, implementation strategies (upper, top-down, and bottom-up) and a productivity analysis which is generous to the CASE cause.

James Ray III (Director, MIS Eckerd Drug Company) commenting on the strategies introduced the concept of "situationally dependent transition":

The Case approach a business chooses depends greatly on their current personnel, the extent to which a formal structured methodology is implemented, and the adequacy of budget for tools and training. I think it will also be affected by management's preferred technique for monitoring the MIS function. Those shops with an eye on old metrics like "lines of code" will tend to steer towards lower CASE first. Those with a focus on customer service and quality will seek out upper CASE first. In all situations, I believe the move to CASE technology will be evolutionary rather than revolutionary, hence the transition.

Mr. Richard Manicom's "pragmatic" view on architected applications is contained in Appendix D. It presents data design limitations in the Upper CASE process. Lower CASE is further analyzed in Appendix E which covers the following topics: productivity matrix, evaluation plan, requirements, and paradox.

Positioning 4GLs in a corporation is the subject of chapter 5. Differences among companies are based more on environmental factors than on technical factors. A decision matrix establishes criteria for defending a factory strategy on 4GLs. No longer does an organization have to become defensive when vendors and consultants call COBOL a poor choice. The paradox of diverse but equally successful strategies is finally reconciled.

However, the debate on the value of 4GLs continues into the 1990s. The luster of 4GLs has been dimmed by lower Case. Does an opportunity exist to merge the non-procedure aspects of an established 4GL with a lower Case product providing COBOL source code? Possibly, but the development effort is substantial.

The latest "fad" is object oriented programming system (OOPS) which promises higher productivity (both in development and maintenance) and is effective for graphics. The OOPS approach is the opposite of separating data from programs—an MIS mission over the past 10 years. In OOPS, the concept is to join data and program code, such as, validation and update logic—a form of standardization. Will OPPS move into the mainstream of business programming? Probably not, although it may be used for programming the Graphic User Interface (GUI) in the client/server environment.

As an introduction to Chapter 6 on expert systems (ES), consider the following quote:

Companies who find and develop knowledge-based applications first will retain their competitive edge in the marketplace.

ES, however, may not be readily integrated into the applications developed by the Software Factory. Rather, the popular ES concept will find acceptance in user organizations and vendor products supporting the software development process. The chapter presents a quiz to facilitate the definition of ES characteristics.

CHAPTER **4**

*CASE Strategies**

Management Information System Vice President: It is known the company is emphasing productivity in all divisions. To survive as a corporation, everyone must become more productive.

Systems Development Director: MIS will support the corporate direction. The new on-line credit system will not only improve productivity, but also it provides a competitive advantage.

MIS VP: Yes, the Business System Planning (BSP) identified credit validation as an opportunity. But, within the department what is happening to reduce the time required to develop systems?

S/D Dir: Over the years the Systems Development Life Cycle (SDLC) has been modified significantly with design standards, implementation checklists, on-line software tools and training.

MIS VP: Have these techniques doubled productivity?

S/D Dir: Probably not, maybe a 25 to 30 percent improvement over the past five years.

*Adapted from Johnson, James R. "Case Strategies", *Main Frame Journal* (June 1990), pp. 24–32.

MIS VP: I have read a revolutionary change that may improve productivity by a factor of five is imminent. Is it called computer engineering?

S/D Dir: Yes, Computer Aided Software Engineering (CASE) products have been under study by our staff for about a year and a report will be published soon. But, I am not convinced it is a revolution. I remember the last three revolutions: database, structured methods and 4GLs. Separating data from programs never did simplify development or maintenance as anticipated; although, standardizing I/O interfaces, concurrent batch and online processing and real-time recovery were major benefits of database. The structured programming method definitely improved the ability to test and maintain programs, but the manual structured design approach actually decreased productivity, therefore, the techniques were discontinued. Not long after those efforts, maybe seven or eight years ago, two production systems with 4GLs were installed. They were complex, requiring extensive procedure code which created a maintenance nightmare. The programs were finally converted to COBOL.

MIS VP: Do not forget how 4GL knowledge accelerated the end-user computing program.

S/D Dir: As with each of the "revolutionary technologies," ancillary benefits were realized.

MIS VP: I remember the promises and the results, but I thought CASE addresses deficiencies of previous failures by providing a comprehensive repository, PC diagramming aids and COBOL code.

S/D Dir: Yes, the claims are based on new integrated technology.

MIS VP: Then increased productivity will result in both development and maintenance, right?

S/D Dir: Yes, the literature claims dramatic improvements in both areas.

MIS VP: What is the principle?

S/D Dir: For development, a PC with graphics is used to generate diagrams explaining and documenting the system. To elim-

FIGURE 4.1 Life cycle definition.

Phase	*Percent Of Project*	*Tasks*
I. Analysis	5 to 15	Define business functions: what is to be done Understand problems with existing system Produce high-level design of proposed system Decompose the process Define general data needs Analyze organization and system interfaces Document benefits
II. Design	25 to 35	Define normal processing: how system will work Define exception processing Specify equipment Define specific data structures Design actual interface, inputs and outputs
III. Implementation	50 to 70	Programming Testing (unit, integrated, user acceptance) Training Conversion
IV. Maintenance		Enhancements Technical upgrades Functional additions Correcting design flaws

inate programming, a code generator uses action diagrams, a form of pseudo code, to produce COBOL programs. Subsquent maintenance is via the diagrams so understanding detailed COBOL code is not necessary. Analysts, in effect, replace programmers.

MIS VP: Sounds interesting, applying computer technology to the software development process. What is the risk?

S/D Dir: The software investment is more than $200,000 and PC workstations are required for the entire staff. There is risk because the success stories are scarce and for less complex environments.

MIS VP: Your study has lasted more than a year, what are the leading products?

S/D Dir: The issue is more complex than just rating product capabilities. First, it is necessary to understand the inherent problems or barriers to productivity.

Similar conversations may be typical in everyone's organization. This article may provide a framework for comparing different strategies. After brief definitions and comments on the article's scope, inherent productivity barriers are presented for life cycle phases. Then, upper and lower CASE capabilities are summarized. The merits of four CASE strategies in context with the inherent barriers are followed by matching products to strategies and, finally, productivity gains are stated.

DEFINITIONS

A recent article on managing projects concluded that management (establishing vision, commitment, communication, lead-

FIGURE 4.2 Inherent barriers.

Phase	*Symptom*	*Inherent Barriers*
I. Analysis	Missing or incorrect requirements	Current and future needs are unknown
II. Design	Lack of system integration—the spaghetti chart	Compromise due to complexity restrict integration
III. Implementation	Slow, error-prone process of programming	Standardization is required for code reuse
IV. Maintenance	Required 70 to 80 percent of resources	Business change creates maintenance

FIGURE 4.3 Application interfaces.

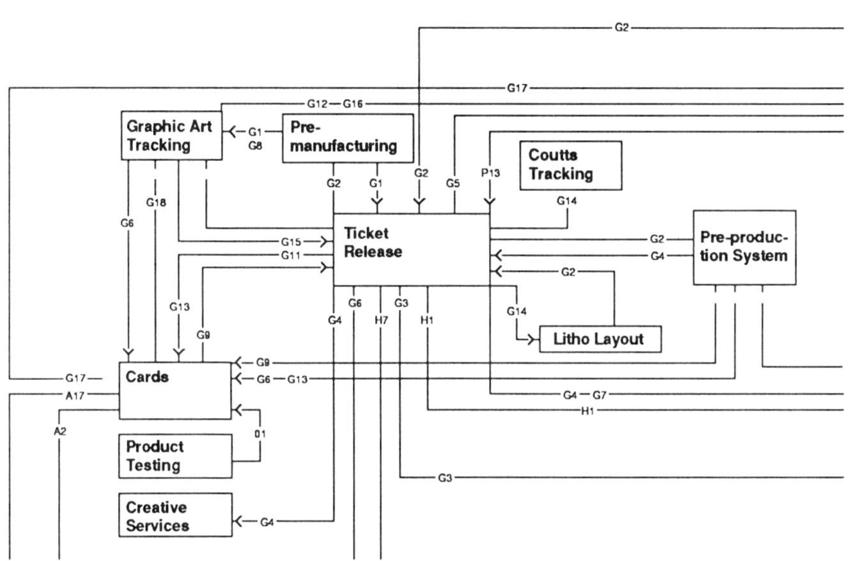

ership and risk) was the most critical factor in the success of a project. Other factors such as human resource, methodology and techniques were secondary. The context was success or failure. The main topic of this article is productivity within the Systems Development Life Cycle (SDLC), a subset of project success or failure and a more focused topic concerned with methodology and techniques. Everyone agrees management must be involved, but controversy surrounds the secondary issues. How many agree on what productivity gains are possible or what CASE strategy to pursue?

This analysis applies to large COBOL mainframe-based operations, organizations that build and maintain backbone and strategic corporate systems for functional areas like finance, marketing, order processing, distribution, personnel and manufacturing. It does not apply to small organizations, research, end user, information centers or academic situations. The strategy of purchased software, which impacts development and maintenance productivity, is also outside of the scope. Furthermore, the term *system* has the following descriptive attributes: documented, integrated, significant number of data fields, complex processing, used by multiple people, major effort to develop two-plus man years, significant number of input/output (screens, reports and so on). And last, assume the SDLC consists of four phases as defined by Figure 4.1: analysis, design, implementation and maintenance.

PRODUCTIVITY SYMPTOMS AND INHERENT BARRIERS

Analysis

Each life cycle phase has characteristic symptoms reducing productivity as shown in Figure 4.2. For the analysis phase, missing or incorrect requirements is the symptom. The implied assumption is that users know what they need, not just in the current environment but also in the future environment. It assumes a design team, with appropriate tools, can correctly define the "right" system (sometimes labeled a quality system). However, the inherent barrier, unknown needs, prevents complete success. Fourteen years ago Fred Brooks explained this principle in his book "The Mythical Man-Month:"

> *Where new system concept or new technology is used, one has to build a system to throw away, for even the best planning is not so omniscient as to get it right the first time. The management question, therefore, is not whether to build a pilot system and throw it away. You will do that. The only question is whether to plan in advance to build a throwaway, or to promise to deliver the throwaway to customers. Seen this way, the answer is much clearer. . . . Hence plan to throw one away; you will, anyhow.*

Have the new CASE technologies invalidated this principle? This question is addressed in the Strategies section.

Design

The term *spaghetti* has been used to describe drawings of application system interfaces, data passing within and among systems. See Figure 4.3 for a subset of an actual example (each connecting line is a file or database). The productivity symptom, lack of integration, reflects the absence of global corporate system architecture. But the inherent barrier is design complexity and compromise in the design process. Integration of corporate systems involves hundreds of files (databases), thousands of programs and tens of thousands of data elements—a complex situation. Additionally, since systems have 5- to 10-year lives, new applications must interface with a variety of "old" systems. To accomodate inconsistencies, design compromise becomes the rule rather than the exception.

Implementation

The implementation phase is dominated by programming and testing. The slow, error-prone programming process is the productivity symptom. However, the inherent barrier is standardization, the basis for reusable code. The ultimate code reuser is a non-procedural language, the key to 4GL's success. Procedural approaches, classified primarily as code generators, utilize abbreviated symbols and macro statements (common code, driven by parameters) to achieve code reuse. Cloning code, made possible by on-line editors, has a disadvantage in the maintenance phase since a common source does not exist. To explain why standardization is difficult to implement, consider the following specific areas:

- Navigation or menu transportation from screen to screen
- Screen layout or position of dates, messages, transaction numbers and so on
- Program Function (PF) key usage or scrolling, menu return and so on
- Error processing and presentation or message format, location, stacking and so on
- Table handling or building, adding, deleting, displaying, accessing, validating and so on
- Program architecture or processing cycle or sequence, such as receive screen, validate fields, update and so on.

In large shops with separate teams supporting different business applications, it is difficult to support standardization because each team has its own opinion about handling user interface and other internal programming tasks. Enforcing these standards without automation is an unrealistic management goal.

Maintenance

Most corporations devote 70 to 80 percent of their analyst and programmer resources to maintenance, the task of modifying existing systems. The connotation of this symptom is poor designs which create systems that are difficult and time consuming to change. However, the symptom is misleading since the majority of maintenance requests support "business change" unanticipated during design (which may have occurred months or years earlier).

Flexible systems handle routine changes such as new pay scales and discount rates via external tables, but few systems are flexible enough to incorporate all aspects of change related to products, organization or distribution. In other words, maintenance, considered mundane by some, is strategically supporting the corporation.

FIGURE 4.4 Four strategies.

CASE Strategy	*Why*
1. Wait	Risky, major investment, extensive training required on-line tools have already improved productivity, CASE products not mature, do not believe benefits
2. Use upper CASE for analysis and design	Believe structured methodology will produce correct design saving time in implementation and maintenance
3. Select top-down CASE for SDLC	Same as above Also, believe link from upper to lower saves considerable effort Maintenance via CASE tool
4. Select bottom-up CASE and prototyping for SDLC	Believe extensive prototyping produces best design Betting on non-procedural improvements Maintenance via CASE tool

CASE Classification

The industry classifies CASE tools as upper and lower. The upper CASE products use PC workstations to automate creation of structured diagrams used in the analysis and design phase. Some examples for data are data model, entity-relationships diagrams and data flow diagrams. Other examples for process are functional decomposition, structure charts and action diagrams.

The rules and syntax to produce a diagram depend on the particular method adopted: Yourden, Jackson, Martin, Constantine and so on. Each method has strengths and weaknesses. Criteria for comparison include: emphasis of data or process; dynamic versus static representation showing sequence of events; relational data versus hierarchical formats; design validation/error checking (one method claims mathematically provable design). Historically, the structure methods introduced in the 1970s lost popularity because the manual effort decreased productivity. However, the powerful PC tools (mouse, windows, menus, graphics) of upper CASE products eliminate the manual effort, especially for changes.

The lower CASE products, host-based code generators, create executable COBOL code from abbreviated COBOL, store reusable code called macros in repositories and utilize non-procedural concepts. Since host-based, the 3270 technology is the input tool. Although PC versions are available, compatibility objectives limit the exploitation of powerful PC tools.

Striving for a product impacting the entire life cycle, major CASE vendors are searching for complementary products to form a conprehensive tool—a tool whree outputs, such as diagrams, serve as inputs to subsequent activities, eliminating duplication of effort within the life cycle.

STRATEGIES

There are basically four CASE strategies available to an organization developing software:

1. Wait for the products to mature
2. Implement upper CASE for design and analysis
3. Select top down CASE for the entire SDLC

4. Select bottom-up CASE which emphasizes prototyping for the entire life cycle.

The strategies and summary logic are shown in Figure 4.4. Surprisingly the word "believe" is used as a criteria for selection. Arguments for strategies reveal controversial questions: is the risk of implementing CASE significant, do structured methods improve design, can extensive prototyping save time, does CASE impact maintenance?

Wait

A conservative strategy is to do nothing. Wait until CASE tools have a proven track record. Wait until the products evolve. One argument is that strategic corporate systems have been, and will continue to be, installed with existing life-cycle methods. Also, the hardware, software and training resources are expensive. Workstations range form $10,000 to $15,000 per person and low-code generators are in excess of $200,000. Other arguments supporting the wait strategy might be the unproven success of structured technologies: does quality design result, can interfaces be simplified with data modeling and architecture charts, does logical design convert to physical design, is maintenance less? And finally, have structured enthusiasts created "neat stuff" so that the color coded diagrams have become the end itself rather than a means to an end.

Implement Upper CASE

Proponents of this strategy believe it is possible to apply an engineering approach to analysis and design. Historically, the manual effort restricted the methodology, which now supports both data and process diagramming. The engineering approach, a thorough analysis of business functions, identifies true needs. The diagramming tools clarify intrinsic business requirements, producing a quality system. Efforts on architecture simplify spaghetti charts and thus reduce maintenance efforts. Applied correctly, the methodology provides both a global and application architecture. This architecture is analogous to a city providing for growth with roads, utilities and so on. The logical models and database supporting business functions remain stable for the critical infrastructure systems. The upper CASE tools provide for validation of the design and cross checking for completeness and accuracy. Also, graphics are like pictures, they allow users to quickly understand complex issues. Other productivity aids include automatic documentation and a dictionary or repository.

Select Top-Down CASE

The term *top-down* is defined as an integrated upper and lower CASE with the upper CASE driving the SDLC. All the advantages listed for upper CASE are applicable. For programming, specification charts called action diagrams are translated by a code generator to COBOL. This procedural process allows for code reuse via a repository that references macro statements. Thus, tools to accomplish the inherent problem of standardization are provided. Productivity is further improved by linking relevant analysis and design diagrams to programming and testing; however, not all diagrams contain detail, such as data names, required during implementation. Maintenance is easier because changes are made at a higher level avoiding the archaic programming process. Code directories and pretested modules provide the leverage.

Select Bottom-Up CASE

The term bottom-up CASE defines a strategy emanating from lower CASE products. It expands the prototyping capabilities of code generators into the design and analysis phase. Proponents of prototyping believe users must interact with the system in a live environment before real needs are known. Abstract models are of limited value. They subscribe to the "plan-to-throw-one-away" philosophy. Arguing for working models and the iterative process, prototypers criticize structure methodologies as non-intuitive. For example, terms such as logical models, isomorphic mapping, objects, attributes, entries, absolute reference and so on may confuse rather than clarify the issue.

The bottom-up approach does not preclude corporate data

models which may be part of a business system plan preceding the analysis phase. This issue is independent of the top-down or bottom-up approach. The immediate value of corporate data modeling depends on when (number of years) existing systems can be integrated into a new architecture.

The linkage between design and programming with prototyping is straightforward since an abbreviated COBOL language with supporting macros is used throughout the SDLC. Bottom-up CASE also supports non-procedure programming, the ultimate concept in code reuse, for the less complex system processing.

On the negative side, an acknowledged disadvantage of prototyping is the lack of structure involved in the entire process. Also, prototyping does not emphasize design integration. Obviously, strategies three and four are not completely mutually exclusive; top-down CASE may use prototyping and bottom-up CASE may include data and process diagramming. The distinction is one of emphasis or priority.

PRODUCTIVITY

Possible productivity improvements for each strategy are shown in Figure 4.5 (based on a ten man-year project with a seven-year life).

FIGURE 4.5 Productivity.

			Strategy (Man Years)		
	1990 Percent Dev Effort	*1990 Man Years*	*Upper CASE*	*Top Down Case*	*Bottom Up CASE*
Analysis	5 to 15	1	1	1	1
Design	25 to 35	3	4	4	2
Implementation	50 to 70	6	5	2	3
	100	10	10	7	6
Maintenance for seven years		14	12	8	9

For the 1990 project, development effort is allocated by phase as follows: analysis 10 percent, design 30 percent and implementation 60 percent. Reflecting two man years of maintenance per year for each ten man years of development, the fourteen man years of maintenance covers a seven-year system life. It provides personnel for basic support and enhancements due to business change.

As the numbers reflect, each strategy favorably impacts productivity although by different amounts and for different reasons. Some would argue that CASE strategies impact the analysis phase, however since the chart is in whole numbers and since the phase comprises only 10 percent of the effort, the impact is ignored. Continuing to explain the chart, note the off-setting man years using upper CASE. Compensating for the design time increase was an equal decrease in the implementation phase. This is because a more rigorous design simplifies the programming and testing aspects of implementation. Using similar logic, maintenance resources are also less by two man years or 14 percent.

The top-down CASE strategy shows a remarkable reduction in the implementation phase, six to two man years. In addition to cross checking, dictionary capabilities and automated validation, the specification language generates pretested code, saving both programming and testing time. Thus, the third strategy results in a 30 percent productivity improvement for project development. The maintenance effort is reduced in a similar manner based on the high-level specification language.

The bottom-up CASE approach reduces documentation cutting design time from the 1990 level. The programming improvement is less than top-down CASE because with prototyping the same emphasis is not devoted to developing a thorough design. The nine man years of maintenance is a 36 percent reduction over 1990 efforts but one man year greater than with top-down CASE which predicts a more integrated system. In all strategies, the amount of maintenance is not reduced since it is based on business change, but rather, the time to perform maintenance is reduced.

PRODUCTS

Selected products supporting CASE strategies are shown in Fig. 4.6. Upper CASE products run on PCs as part of an analyst workbench which may include word processing, electronic mail and other tools. Generally, the products support the six data and process charts previously listed although syntax varies by vendors.

Only a few comprehensive top-down CASE products exist. The difficulty is providing a link that effectively utilizes upper CASE diagrams and documentation in the implementation and maintenance phase.

In the future, host-based products used for bottom-up CASE may develop links to existing upper CASE products or develop their own diagramming tools.

CONCLUSION

In summary, productivity for development ranged from zero to 40 percent, not a factor of two or five times as some vendors claim. The greatest productivity gains were within the implementation phase. The seven-year maintenance effort (which exceeds the development effort for every strategy), showed equivalent improvement ranging from 14 to 43 percent.

MIS VP: Thanks for the update. I see why the analysis has taken so long. It is more than just comparing products, it involves understanding the inherent productivity barriers.

S/D Dir: Yes and there is controversy between structured methodologies and the prototyping philosophy.

MIS VP: There is no quick fix. Productivity projections, although significant, will not revolutionize the industry. What is the next step?

S/D Dir: The next step is selecting a strategy.

MIS VP: Is it possible to use different strategies in different areas instead of one strategy?

S/D Dir: Combining strategies is possible, but not receommended. One primary strategy is the most desirable.

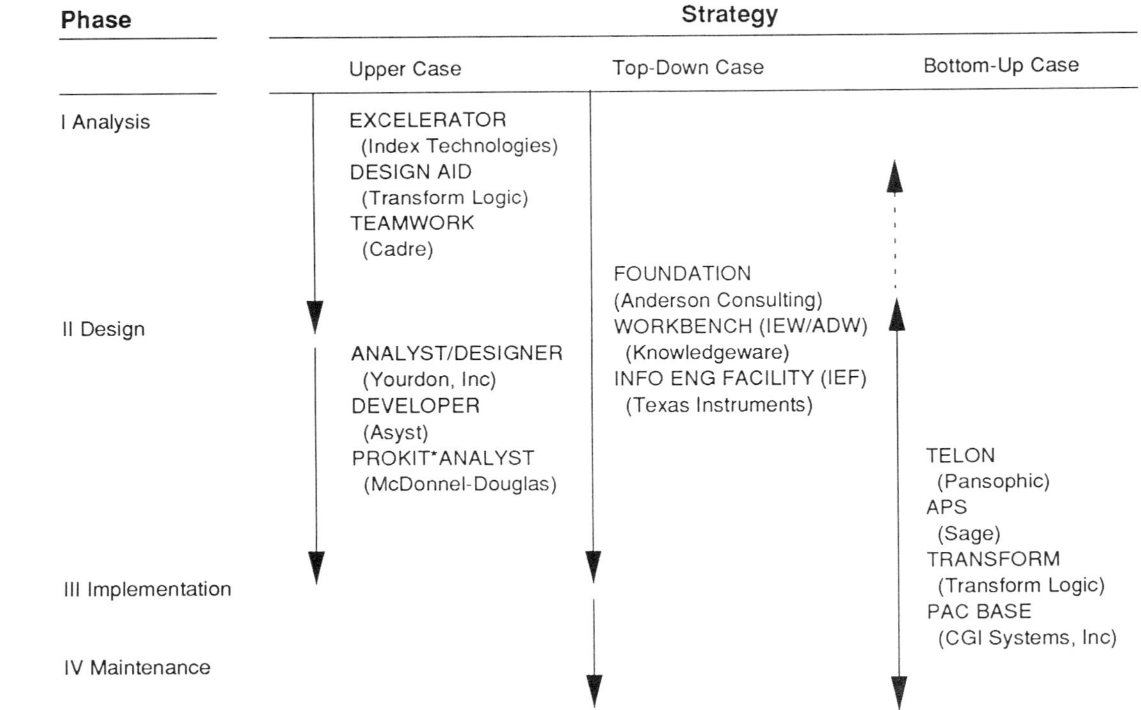

Figure 4.6 Selected Products

MIS VP: Which strategy is recommended?

S/D Dir: Even after the analysis the staff is not in agreement—there are votes for each strategy. But I think . . .

REFERENCES

Chantico Publishing Company. *Case: The Potential and Pitfalls.* QED Information Sciences, Inc., Wellesley, MA. 1989

McClure, Carma. *Case Is Software Automation*, Prentice Hall, Englewood Cliffs, N.J., 1989

Anderson Consulting. *Foundations of Business Systems*, Dryden Press, Orlando, Florida, 1989

Manicom, Richard. "The Dangers of 'Architectured' Applications" Guide 75 Session MP7064, Nov. 9, 1989

CHAPTER 5

*Fourth-Generation Languages (4GLs)**

MIS vice-president: We have been researching fourth-generation languages (4GLs) and may soon implement the selected product for all development. I would like you to review our logic and comment on the proposed strategy.

Consultant: What have you learned from the research?

MIS vice-president: Well, first, improving productivity during the development cycle is a high priority. A pilot project indicated a 3:1 productivity gain over COBOL, our standard procedural language. Also, maintenance is now almost 60 percent of the system development resource; a 4GL should reduce the percent significantly.

Consultant: Anything else?

MIS vice-president: Yes, 4GL capabilities have matured. In addition to ad hoc reporting, they now support graphics, simulation,

*Adapted from Johnson, James R. "Users Fine-Tune 4GL Strategies." *Computerworld* (March 31, 1986), 65–71.

and database update. Also, we feel CPU consumption can be controlled via tuning.

Consultant: Do your end users write their own reports?

MIS vice-president: Yes, most do, and we support this trend.

Consultant: Do end users develop small, less-than-one-man-year systems on their own with a 4GL?

MIS vice-president: Yes, in most areas.

Consultant: Are your corporate applications highly integrated and tailored?

MIS vice-president: Yes, very much so. You should see our system integration chart showing all the data and file interfaces.

Consultant: How about productivity aids for your standard procedural language—are they extensively developed?

MIS vice-president: We have a state-of-the-art operation utilizing on-line edit, compile and debug. Structured code has been used for years, and code is copied whenever possible.

But your questions don't relate to the assignment I hired you for. They are organizational issues. Let's talk about whether or not we should use a 4GL for all future applications based on technical factors such as language capability, CPU requirements and productivity.

Consultant: Let me explain my logic . . .

This dialogue introduces factors normally not related to an MIS division's 4GL strategy. Are the consultant's questions about user responsibility, system integration and existing productivity techniques legitimate? Why are there no follow-up questions on the traditional issues of development productivity and CPU consumption?

Since our 4GL strategy is conservative, allowing only one programming group to use a 4GL, a project was initiated to define the factors influencing 4GL strategies. The results would hopefully reconcile our rule of limited use with other strategies employing a more liberal deployment of 4GLs.

A decision matrix, a tool for developing or refining a 4GL

strategy, can aid the analysis of various strategic factors, such as programmer and maintenance productivity and CPU and language capabilities. This matrix allows diverse strategies for different corporations and concludes that organizational issues, not technical ones, dominate the strategy selection.

Our experience is based on UFO Development (Martin Marietta Data Systems), work with Focus (Information Builders, Inc.), extensive end-user support of Report Writing with Mark IV (Informatics), and work with Interactive Financial Planning System (Execucom Systems Corp.)

Personal experiences were supplemented by a survey of MIS managers with a variety of responsibilities. The survey obtained data and comments on languages used, percent of MIS staff using 4GLs, CPU concerns, strategies for employing 4GLs, and maintenance requirements. The emphasis centered on technology issues, since those were judged to be of primary importance at the time.

The companies selected possess varying degrees of 4GL experience. Fifteen companies returned the completed form, including American Cyanamid Co.; Bell Canada; Bethlehem Steel Corp.; Burlington Industries, Inc.; Coca-Cola Co.; Duke Power Co.; Johnson & Johnson; Monsanto Co.; and Ralston Purina Co. The survey base is composed of relatively large companies, more than half reported systems development staffs of more than 100 people.

After reflecting on the survey's diversity, a pattern emerged that related the strategies used with the technical and organizational environment of each company. This view was verified during a seminar presentation of the survey results. More than 50 companies participated in the group discussions; representative comments are presented here.

VARIETY OF STRATEGIES

4GL strategies define who, when, and how the languages are used in a corporation. In the course of the project, there emerged a collection of strategic rules, such as the following:

- Use packages first, 4GLs second and no 3GLs.
- Wait for fifth-generation languages while investing in 3GLs productivity aids.

FIGURE 5.1. A 4GL strategy decision matrix. The questions in this decision matrix consider technical, MIS, and corporate factors that influence decisions to use a 4GL. Depending on a yes or no answer, recommendations for devising strategies are given.

Technical Issues	*Yes*	*No*
Is development time a priority? Is maintenance consuming an increasing percent of the staff?	System complexity, as defined by percent of procedure code, is the key variable vs. a yes or no answer. For simple and some more complex systems, a 4GL may reduce development time and maintenance requirements.	
Is CPU consumption a main criterion?	Tuning is possible except in very high-volume situations.	Should be considered
Are the language capabilities comprehensive? Each language has strengths, but many cover total MIS requirements (ad hoc reporting, file definition, graphics, batch reporting, screen generation).	May be used for entire system.	Utilize language's strength (ad hoc reporting, grapics, screen generation and so on).

MIS Organization Issues	*Yes*	*No*
Are applications highly integrated?	Language not used to greatest advantage with highly integrated systems.	Consider language for independent applications.
Limited prototyping environment?	Benefits limited.	Prototyping is good use of language.

FIGURE 5.1. Continued

MIS Organization Issues	*Yes*	*No*
Are multiple productivity aids implemented for existing procedural language?	Benefits reduced.	Potential for improved productivity.
Corporate Organizational Issues	*Yes*	*No*
Do end users write their own reports (batch or on-line)?	Since language utilized by end users, MIS need minimized.	MIS should consider language for reports.
Do end users develop and install small systems (less than one man-year) with the language?	Since language utilized by end users, MIS need minimized.	MIS should consider language for small systems.
Do end users demand tailored systems?	Not recommended for complex systems.	Consider for straightforward systems.
Is obtaining an additional CPU a problem?	Not recommended.	Should be considered.

- Separate all report-writing functions organizationally, and employ a 4GL for this purpose.
- Use a 3GL for complex reports and batch processing and a 4GL for simple and medium reports.
- Make decisions on 4GLs on a system-by-system basis, using processing characteristics as the criteria.

As expected, the survey confirms that a variety of strategies exist among corporations: Seven organizations reported less than 20 percent of the staff using 4GLs, while four organizations noted more than 60 percent of the staff using a 4GL. Why the disparity occurs—a more difficult question—was not answered directly by the survey.

As an example of the selection process, consider some survey responses to the question, "What is the basis for determining if an application should be written in a 4GL?"

In our installation, all new applications are fourth-generation or higher level languages unless purchased.

The MIS staff has a list of strengths and weaknesses for the 4GL tools. The MIS staff also consults with the development center to make appropriate language selections.

Judgment based on apparent size and complexity of application. Use limited strictly to simple applications.

Obviously, among corporations, a spectrum of 4GL strategies exists—from developing all applications in a 4GL to limited or no use of those languages. Who is right? What are the relevant factors? Users trying to determine the correct fourth-generation strategy to use should consider the following criteria.

DECISION MATRIX (Figure 5.1)

Is development time a priority? 4GL development productivity is dictated by the amount of procedure code required. 4GLs dramatically reduce development time for simple applications, but this advantage decreases as more procedure code is required. Thus, to argue delivery time without considering the complexity of development is misleading.

Is maintenance consuming an increasing percent of the staff? Maintenance productivity follows a similar pattern as that of determining development time.

In James Martin's book *Application Development Without Programmers* (The Telecom Library, New York, 1982), a 58-line COBOL program calculating the mean of a set of numbers is replaced by one line of Nomad code: READ DIGITS LIST AVG (DIGITS) —an impressive demonstration of the power of 4GL nonprocedural code. However, another side to the productivity issue exists that is substantiated by our experiences, the survey, and other sources.

Basically, 4GL productivity, either in development or support, is dependent on the amount and clarity of the procedure code, code necessary when the automatic parameters are not sufficient.

The key 4GL variable, complexity, is the ratio of procedure code to total code required for the program or system. For simpler systems, 4GL productivity considerably exceeds COBOL; many documented projects support a productivity ratio of 5:1.

As the ratio of procedure code to total code, or complexity, increases, the 4GL advantage diminishes; for complex applications, COBOL, because of its flexibility and structure, rates higher in productivity.

The development project productivity chart (see Figure 5.2) graphs productivity ranges for 4GLs and COBOL, the predominant 3GL. The COBOL lines of code are realistic and generally substantiated by comparisons with other corporations and available literature.

The average number of lines of code per man-day for all projects is 75. This relatively high value is obtained by using productivity aids such as on-line compile, on-line debug, copied code, and subsecond response time.

Complexity for COBOL is a relative measure (since it is 100 percent procedure code) based on a combination of project innovation, technology, and size. Average productivity increases 50 percent on each step from complex (50 lines of code) to medium (75 lines) to simple (112 lines).

The most important survey response emphasizes this point: Use 4GLs for simple applications. Eight companies indicate that the basis for writing an application in a 4GL is simplicity. Six responses to the question, "Do you feel programs written in 4GL are easily supported?" affirmed, "Yes, if they are simple." Other companies noted that productivity with 4GL depends on complexity:

Varying degrees of productivity can be realized, depending on the complexity of applications. . . . 4GLs were not intended to be used for complex applications.

Complex requests are very difficult to support when problems arise or enhancements are requested.

FIGURE 5.2. Development project productivity chart. As the complexity of program development increases, the fourth-generation language advantage diminishes.

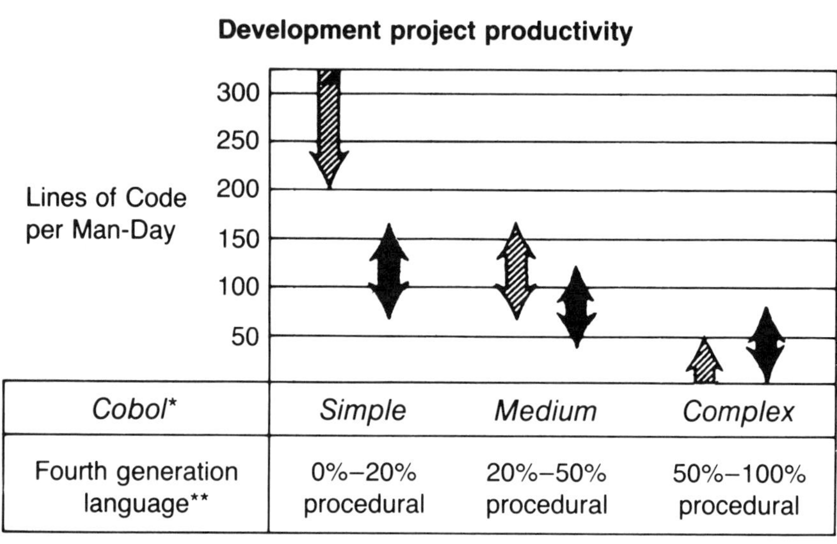

*COBOL complexity based on relative difficulty
**Fourth-generation language complexity: Percent of procedure code to total code

If the system is complex, the productivity gains will be less.

This is not the first time this concept has been documented. An October 1984 study by Framingham, Mass.-based market research firm International Data Corp., "Fourth-Generation Language: Information Generators to Meet Information Needs," states that large integrated systems required expert skill for 4GLs but lesser skill for COBOL.

It further states, "Fourth-generation languages and COBOL are fundamentally different, and organizations should not make the mistake of viewing these two types of programming methods as interchangeable."

A presentation by the Guide IBM users group included a

similar chart showing the productivity of 4GLs (IBM's DMS and ADF) decreasing with increased complexity, and complex 4GL applications having less productivity than COBOL. Thus, complexity is the significant variable determining productivity within the development and maintenance process.

CONSUMPTION AN OPEN ISSUE

Is CPU consumption a main criterion? The next technical factor, CPU consumption, introduces controversy as illustrated by the following survey comments:

Ungoverned usage of fourth-generation language in both MIS and user areas has dramatic impact on CPU resources. Further, the implications of this usage for future information activities create concern regarding our ability to integrate systems effectively.

Minor machine overheads are far overshadowed by productivity gains.

CPU consumption is an open issue, especially for high-volume transactions. One study concludes that 10 end users running Focus simultaneously consume 76 percent of an IBM 3081 Model G's CPU capacity, an uncomfortable result for computer operations managers.

On the other hand, eight survey respondents said they do not experience excessive 4GL CPU use. Only four companies noted CPU consumption as a problem. The paradox can be explained by one of the following:

- Performance tuning is possible in most situations.
- Simple programs inherently use small amounts of CPU resources.
- In some environments, the CPU resource is not a constraint.

Assuming the survey presents a representative sample, excessive CPU use normally does not constitute a problem unless transaction volumes are extreme.

STRENGTHS AND WEAKNESSES

Are the 4GL capabilities comprehensive—each language has strengths, but many cover total MIS requirements? Although most popular 4GLs can be used to build complete systems, each language possesses strengths and weaknesses. Thus, if a comprehensive language is available, entire systems can be developed. If a more limited 4GL is the option, exploit its strengths. For example, on-line screen-painting.

The following languages were considered typical 4GLs: IBM's ADF; Focus; Applied Data Research, Inc.'s Ideal; IFPS; Software AG of North America, Inc.'s Natural; Martin Marietta Data Systems' Ramis II and UFO. Distinguishing 4GLs as application generators, primarily for MIS professionals, or very high-level languages, primarily for end users, may be academic, since almost all 4GLs are examples of both.

The survey did not attempt to document specific 4GL characteristics such as ad hoc query, graphics, simulation, report generation or database update; however, the languages listed generally share four capabilities:

- They allow interactive development and testing.
- They provide nonprocedural (what vs. how) coding.
- They interface with various databases.
- They increase productivity by as much as five times that of COBOL (as measured in function points or equivalent lines of code).

MIS ORGANIZATIONAL ISSUES

MIS organizational issues address application integration, prototyping, and current productivity on 3GLs.

Are applications highly integrated? Extensive integration implies complexity and thus reduces the 4GL advantage.

Limited prototyping environment? Prototyping provides a sound reason for using a 4GL; however, 3GLs may also be used successfully.

Are multiple productivity aids implemented for existing procedural language? For the issue of existing productivity aids, take the extreme example of a relatively small organization, with 30 systems development personnel using batch COBOL, in which the line-of-code productivity falls in the low range for the three complexity levels shown in the project productivity chart.

In this case, potential exists for significant productivity gains, and a 4GL may provide the best approach. Thus, the incremental productivity increase for a 4GL depends on current 3GL productivity.

The training and support aspect of introducing a new language should not be minimized. A critical mass of expertise and cross-training is a requirement. To a degree, the amount of this support argues for a strategy based on organization, such as certain project groups heavily utilizing a 4GL vs. the entire staff using it occasionally.

Two organizational aspects excluded from the decision matrix deserve mention. First, high turnover rate is not considered a factor because it affects all strategies adversely—even packaged software is difficult to maintain without expertise. Second, the negative attitudes of MIS management and programmer/analysts toward technology was not judged valid. Although some argue that MIS personnel do not accept 4GLs based on resistance to change, the results of the survey and subsequent discussions with a variety of corporations do not substantiate this claim. In fact, the opposite may be true—managers and staff may be too quick to change based on inflated expectations.

CORPORATE ISSUES

Do end users write their own reports? Do end users develop and install small systems with a 4GL? The extent of end-user computing is a primary corporate organizational issue. If end users assume responsibility for writing reports and installing small systems, then MIS is responsible for generally complex "backbone/core" systems. Thus, 4GLs are of reduced benefit to MIS but of direct benefit to end users.

Do end users demand tailored systems? If end users expect highly tailored systems from MIS, 4GLs are not recommended because procedure code is required for the tailoring process.

Is obtaining additional CPU a problem? Another issue addresses the corporate philosophy toward computer acquisitions. Does the company provide ample CPU capacity so that utilization is not a primary concern? If so, 4GLs are recommended for simple and medium complex systems.

CHANGING VIEWPOINTS

Although the majority of this discussion examines technical issues, specifically productivity and CPU consumption, the questions on MIS and corporate organizational issues are more important when establishing a successful 4GL strategy.

In major corporations, a continuum of 4GL strategies exists, ranging from less than 5 percent to 100 percent of the programming staff using 4GLs. Traditionally, technical factors preoccupy MIS when searching for a 4GL strategy, but it is now evident that an organization's environment should be the primary influence on corporate 4GL strategy.

Returning to the opening conversation:

Consultant: Now, do you see how my earlier questions relate to your 4GL strategy?

MIS vice-president: Yes, based on my answers to the decision matrix questions, 4GLs are recommended for specific functions such as prototyping.

With our organizational structure and integrated, complex applications, it is best to stay with our 3GL and concentrate on productivity aids. However, at our primary subsidiary, the environment is entirely different.

Consultant: What are its needs?

MIS vice-president: It is growing rapidly and needs a variety of different systems as soon as possible. End users will accept "standard" systems; also, the company has adequate CPU capacity.

Consultant: A strategy of first purchasing packaged software and, when doing so is not possible, developing systems exclusively in 4GL sounds reasonable for the subsidiary.

MIS vice-president: I agree. The right strategy varies depending on the corporate environment. Companies need to analyze technical issues but, more important—the firm's environment—before establishing a strategy.

Consultant: The paradox of diverse but equally successful 4GL strategies finally can be reconciled.

CHAPTER 6

Expert Systems

As stated in the introduction, integrating expert system (ES) concepts into the Software Factory product is difficult (although tools used in the development process itself, such as CASE, will utilize ES concepts). Rather than a factory product, the expert system method is viewed as an end-user tool. To understand this statement, a brief review of the accepted architecture and terms is appropriate (see "Terminology" and Figure 6.1).

It is difficult to precisely define an expert system. If you don't think so, take the quiz below. Assume the generally accepted positioning of expert systems as a subset of Artificial Intelligence (AI), which has been defined as programming computers to achieve human-like capabilities, such as seeing, hearing, and thinking. Expert systems are computer programs that mimic the behavior of an expert solving problems. However, learning, determining relevance, and knowing what they don't know are aspects of AI not ES. The quiz covers only rule-based expert systems (RBES) versus hybrid systems, which historically have required specialized hardware and extensive procedural code.

FIGURE 6.1. Architecture chart for an RBES.

Architecture of an RBES

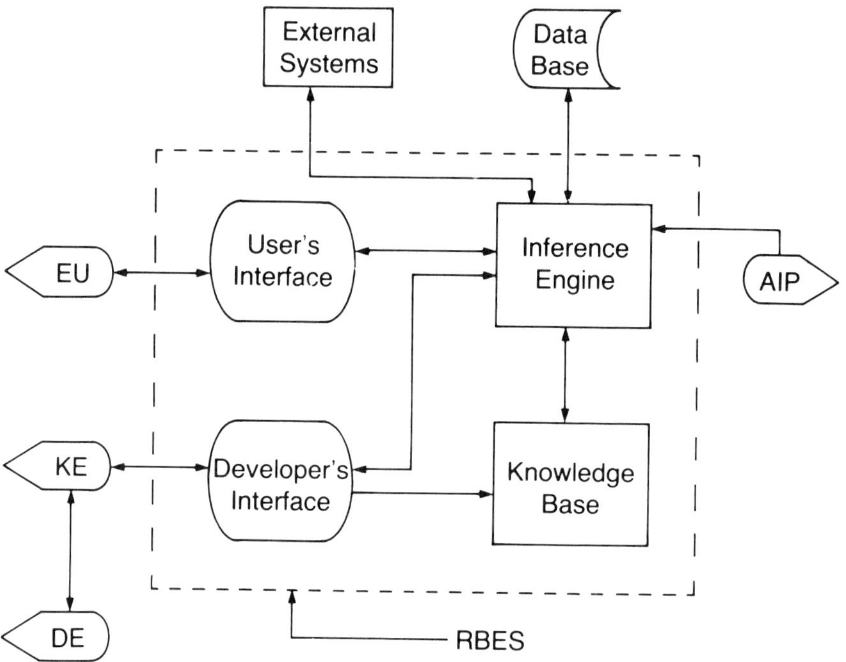

EU = End User, KE = Knowledge Engineer, DE = Domain Expert

AIP = AI Programmer

Rule	A knowledge-representation unit of the form: If A, then B. Rules are used to describe cause-and-effect and rules-of-thumb (heuristic) types of knowledge about a domain (subject). A rule represents a discrete chunk of knowledge.
Knowledge Base (KB)	A required part of RBES consisting of a collection of facts and rules representing expertise about a domain.
Inference Engine (IE)	A required part of RBES that uses the knowledge in the knowledge base to arrive at conclusions.
Domain Expert (DE)	A person with experience and knowledge of a domain (subject, field).

FIGURE 6.1. Continued

Knowledge Engineer (KE)	A person who interacts with the domain expert and represents the domain expert's knowledge in the form of rules and facts.
AI Programmer	A person educated in AI programming methods and languages such as LISP, PROLOG, OPS5, etc.
RBES Shell	Software that consists of an inference engine, a rule-based language for representing knowledge in the knowledge base, and utilities to help a knowledge engineer or domain expert build an RBES without the help of an AI programmer. There is no knowledge base in an expert system shell.
User's Interface	Software providing explanation of why input data are required; software capable of showing the logic used to make a recommendation; software allowing interactive human interface.
Developer's Interface	Software allowing knowledge engineer, domain expert, or, in some cases, end user, to develop or modify the knowledge base incrementally.

QUIZ—Rule-Based Expert Systems (RBES) Characteristics

T F

1. An RBES must be interactive (versus batch).
2. RBES can interact with external traditional systems.
3. An RBES must explain the logic used to arrive at a decision.
4. In RBES, the knowledge base must be separate from the inference engine.
5. Uncertainty or probability is always part of an RBES.
6. RBES must allow for easy incremental expansion (adding more rules or facts to the knowledge base).
7. A commercial software shell is a requirement.
8. A domain expert can read and understand rules without help from a knowledge engineer.
9. RBES may be a trivial application.

10. Traditional MIS applications could be done with an RBES and vice versa.

Before discussing the quiz, consider the objective: defining characteristics distinguishing expert systems from traditional systems. Ideally, a series of questions with Yes or No answers should classify an application as an expert system.

QUIZ Discussion—RBES Characteristics

1. Interactive—False. RBES involving the analysis type of applications (diagnosis, troubleshooting, etc.) are interactive with an on-line human interface. Some applications involving synthesis (design, planning, etc.) are noninteractive, implemented as batch systems.
2. External interfaces—True. The system can interact with external databases, external systems, etc. However, they typically don't interface extensively. This is a weakness of ES software.
3. Explanation—False. The system can explain how it arrived at a specific conclusion or why it is asking for a specific input from the user.
4. Separation—True. The declarative knowedge in the system (knowledge base) is separated from the procedural reasoning process (inference engine). This is a fundamental requirement.
5. Uncertainty—False. It is possible to represent uncertainty in the knowledge base. An inference engine can reason with such uncertain knowledge. However, probability or uncertainty is not required in an RBES. Also, few production systems contain probability.
6. Easy to modify—True. The application can be easily modified by changing some of the facts and rules in the knowledge base.
7. Shell—False. If the inference strategy of an RBES shell is appropriate for the application, a shell can expedite the development process. However, if the application requires a custom inference strategy, then an inference engine will have to be written by an AI programmer. Program efficiency can be a factor in production.
8. Understandability—True. It is easy to understand the knowledge content of the system by simply scanning the facts and rules in the knowledge base.

9. Nontrivial applications—True. Applications are both trivial and nontrivial in complexity and scope. Also, they are relatively unstructured, using primarily non-numeric (symbolic) information.
10. Process—True. The development life cycles for traditional prototype and expert systems are compared below:

Process	*Traditional*	*Prototype*	*RBES*
1. Requirements Definition/Analysis	Formal documents	Formal or informal	Formal or informal
2. Systems Design	Formal documents	Trial and error	Trial and error
3. Programming	Procedural or 4GL	4GL, iterative	Declarative programming, incremental development

The process of building RBES is similar in some respects to prototyping. However, declarative programming is very different from programming in a procedural or fourth generation language (4GL).

Applying the Quiz

The definition of an Expert System is difficult and perhaps arbitrary. The ten characteristics presumably define an expert system. Thus, they should classify applications as expert systems or traditional systems. For example, an order-filling system that decides the size of shipping boxes needed for multiple products of various sizes and weights. User-controlled parameters define the products along with packing constraints. Furthermore, multiple boxes are usually required for one order. An order filler (employee) on the filling floor no longer must decide the size of the box. The system makes the decision consistent with the data provided. Much better utilization of boxes is achieved. The system runs in batch mode with on-line update for all control variables. If the 10 quiz characteristics are applied to this example, two problem areas surface.

First, separation of knowledge base from the inference engine or user understandability (questions 4, 6, and 8). Although this is a gray area, assume the shipping box system passes the expert systems guidelines since users modify the parameter tables independently. The second problem area is the development process (question 10). The system was developed ten years ago by traditional techniques and with COBOL (procedural language). Although the quiz answer said a given application could be done by the traditional process (including prototyping), disagreement is evident when classifying specific systems. In a roundtable meeting, members were divided 50-50 on this issue, one group saying the shipping box system is an expert system, the other disagreeing. During discussions, a surprising concensus evolves:

> *The definition is not dependent on "what" the system does, but rather "who" develops the system or "how" it is developed.*

In other words, any system developed by an expert system team is an expert system, or an application developed with expert system tools (shells or expert system language) is an expert system. If this concept is accepted, the definition is simplified considerably. Perhaps further refining characteristics distinguishing expert systems is counterproductive. Rather, expert systems can be thought of as an innovative technology producing significant benefits on selected applications.

FACTORY APPLICATION

Having acknowledged the difficulty of specifying expert system characteristics, it is appropriate to return to the opening statement—expert systems will integrate slowly into the factory process. The logic is as follows:

- There are two distinct types of ES: large and small. The small applications, run on a PC by users, far outnumber the large applications (sometimes called strategic) which require man-years to develop.
- Personnel in a traditional Software Factory are reluctant to adopt declarative programming; it is simply too different from conventional procedural programming.
- Thus, user groups or special teams, established outside of the factory, will concentrate on developing expert systems.

Ideally, the expert systems technology, specifically declarative programming, should be integrated into the factory process, but, unfortunately, this will be slow to happen. The majority of interest and activity will take place outside of the Software Factory. On large systems, those generally developed by the Software Factory, the expert system "philosophy" of extracting human expertise breaks down protectionist barriers, encouraging individuals to share their knowledge. This is more than a trivial contribution and will be used to advantage by progressive organizations.

REFERENCES

Leonard-Barton, Dorothy, and Suiokla, John J. "Putting Expert Systems to Work." *Harvard Business Review* (March-April) 1988.

Sheil, Beau. "Thinking about Artificial Intelligence." *Harvard Business Review* (July-August 1987).

PART III

Measurement

Productivity equals output divided by resources consumed. Why can't this simplistic equation be used to establish precise productivity figures? If you have studied this area, the obvious problems are known: changing definitions, recording consistent statistics, selecting comparable projects, etc. Our database (Appendix A) was extensive when we started a formal measurement project. Still, the task proved difficult and many myths were discovered as Chapter 7 documents.

The actual 1989 results for our Software Factory are in Appendix F. The productivity documented in Lines of Code (LOC) and Function Points compare favorably with published industry averages. For example, project productivity is over 25,000 LOC per man-year, and the support productivity is 170,000 LOC per person. Of course, comparisons are only valid if based on similar assumptions. Having an eight-year history in one organization with relatively consistent terms allowed a thorough analysis, possibly a unique analysis.

Chapter Eight relates four Japanese just-in-time principles to software quality: line management control, correcting one's own errors, continuous error detection, and easy-to-see quality. Both test plans and post-audits are critical to obtaining quality, and further detail is provided on each topic in Chapters sixteen and seventeen.

Associated with the quality chapter, there are three additional JIT principles that apply to MIS organization and management issues:

- Establish multi-level skills so work groups can operate independently.

- De-emphasize functional organizations placing responsibility with line managers and work groups.
- Use brain power before investing in "Neat" technology.

The classical example of combining multi-level skills is with the analyst and programmer positions. Corporations are divided on the issue, some maintaining two separate groups and others combining the functions. However, the first principle, establishing multilevel skills, supports the concept of one person performing both functions which simplify communication and reduce dependencies.

Functional staffs are established to support technical areas requiring special training. As the function grows each group may have their own agenda and priority. For example: Data Base—normalizing and consolidating data; Development Center—obtaining the latest technological tools; Technical Services—CPU efficiency. Is it possible for service organizations to become self-serving, an obstacle in satisfying the customers' needs? The Japanese think so, their overhead is one-tenth of ours in U.S. manufacturing, but how can functional staffs remain lean in MIS? One way is to standradize complex issues, for example, in the early days all online transactions had to be reviewed by Technical Specialist for design, efficiency, coding structure, etc. As online programming became more common, standards were written and published providing a project team the guidance formerly obtained by technical review. If a functional area's primary objective is to simplify and standardize a procedure for others, different operating philosophy results. Also, queue time, which may represent bottlenecks, exists for functional areas. This queue is each function's "inventory", and inventory adds cycle time.

Inherent with function groups is the propensity to pursue "Neat" stuff, state-of-the-art technology such as expert systems, data design methodology or case tools. Not that neat technology doesn't have its place, but how many conferences do functional groups attend, and how much time is spent searching the world for the best product? Unfortunately, the learning curve on many products is substantial, diverting resources from direct support. The learning represents set-up time which must be minimized for effective operation. The JIT concept asks what can be improved with existing technology by using brain power.

CHAPTER 7

Measuring Performance

After discussing productivity with the corporation's productivity director, the management team estimated a two-week effort to formalize their performance measures. Since the department had concentrated on productivity for years with actual performance statistics available from 1982, the two-week elapsed time was not considered ambitious. However, four and one-half months later, when the new measures were defined, we realized that implementing performance measures is difficult, requiring extensive analysis, and we discovered that existing performance measures were not adequate, requiring formal objectives and plans for improvement. The lessons learned may apply to others, specifically those developing and maintaining software. This is the story of what we learned about productivity measures.

MYTHS

To start the story, consider eight myths associated with performance measures:

1. Performance measures are intuitive.
2. Implementation requires less than three months.

3. All activities should be quantified.
4. Department measures roll down.
5. Improvements automatically follow.
6. Zero defects is the objective.
7. Competing management methodologies are replaced.
8. Corporate benefits are directly linked.

The arguments disputing these myths result from implementing and monitoring nine specific measures in our Software Factory, an environment where over 200 professionals develop, install, and maintain data processing systems.

Myth One. Performance measures are intuitive.

Our definitions of performance measures included four types: productivity, quality, estimating, and other ratios. Until clear definitions were completed, a six-week process, terminology caused considerable confusion. Defined in terms of ratios, the performance measures were as follows:

A. Productivity Measure—an output divided by a resource. The value of this ratio is dependent on how directly the output is related to the resource: the closer the relationship, the better the ratio. The process of producing output is the critical management issue for improving productivity. Examples of outputs for software development: Function Points, Lines Of Code (LOC), programs. Examples of resources: man-days, dollars, employees. Five ratios were defined in this subset as shown on Figure 7.1: Support Productivity, Project Productivity, Function Point Productivity, LOC Productivity, Information Center Productivity.

B. Quality Measure—number not meeting a quality standard divided by total number. Examples: Defects:Total Items, Program Bugs:Total LOC. Two ratios were defined as noted in Figure 7.1: Maintenance UCRs and Installation UCRs. The denominator, Unusual Condition Report (UCR), in this context is simply a program bug causing a system termination. In many discussions of productivity, quality is assumed to remain constant. Measures of quality are indirectly related to the productivity measurement itself, and must be monitored concurrently.

C. Estimates—actual number of resources or outputs meeting estimate (or schedule) divided by the estimate base. Examples: Actual Hours:Budgeted Hours, Projects on Schedule:Total Projects. Two ratios were defined (see Figure 9.1): Schedule Estimate and Budget Estimate. Estimating is also related to productivity, but is based on expectations and not necessarily improving output. It should remain constant or improve as productivity goes up.

D. Other—influencing factors related to productivity; actual divided by goal/target. Examples: Staff Turnover:Target, Training Hours:Target. No ratios for this subset were defined.

In the nine performance measures, only tangible data were used. It is, of course, possible to incorporate opinions and other

FIGURE 7.1. 1989 Performance measure general and specific objectives.

Performance Measure			*General Objective*	*1989 Specific Objective*
A. Productivity				
1. Support Productivity	=	Total LOC / Equiv Support Staff	Increase	160,000
2. Project Productivity	=	Project LOC Implem / Project Man-Years	Maintain or Increase	25,000
3. Function Point Productivity	=	Function Points / Project Man-Days	Increase	.9
4. LOC Productivity	=	LOC Activity / Equiv Enhance/Dev Staff	Increase	22,000
5. Info Center Productivity	=	Function Pt / Programming Man-Days	Increase	12.0
B. Quality				
1. Maintenance UCRs	=	Total LOC / Tot UCR Cnt — Proj UCRs	Maintain or Increase	11,000
2. Project UCRs	=	Project LOC Implem / Project UCRs	Maintain or Increase	7,500
C. Estimating				
1. Schedule Estimate	=	Projects On or Ahead Schedule / Total Projects	Increase	80%
2. Budget Estimate	=	Projects On or Under Budget / Total Projects	Increase	80%

subjective data. Another item avoided was dollarizing the resources. Instead, user man-days or -hours were used. Converting to dollars introduces inflation, an additional complexity. Also, to cover all costs, software and hardware dollars would have to be included. This involves depreciation, leases, rental agreements, etc., and would further complicate the calculation.

All our measures were formally recorded yearly; however, UCR counts for maintenance and projects were monitored monthly as they occurred in net amounts versus ratios. In The Factory it is not possible to link all measures to a month-by-month cycle since implementations occur throughout the year.

Myth Two. Implementation requires less than 3 months.

After six weeks, definitions existed, but it was obvious other steps followed. Over the next four months, specific measures were established, data were analyzed, objectives were set, and plans for improving ratios documented. This effort was longer than anticipated; however, implementation could be significantly longer if consistent output/resource data is not available. In our factory, years had been devoted to refining definitions of the two outputs, Function Points and Lines of Codes. A description of our Function Point approach is documented in Chapter 12.

Historically, monitoring LOC has received considerable criticism; however, if recording rules are consistent and if only one language is used, COBOL in our organization, then LOC is considered a reasonable measure of output. Collection simplicity is one inherent advantage, with no separate calculations needed. In fact, the collection of data may be automated. Although the LOC definition was calculated with minor variations for three measures (Numbers A1, 2, and 4), the general intent is as follows:

> All source statements (physical lines of code) including comments for production programs (excludes conversion and test programs).

Also, an existing time-reporting system isolated the resource (productivity ratio denominator, expressed in man-days) as project, maintenance, or enhancement time. With this data available, defining terms, setting objectives, and documenting an improvement plan were possible in four to five months. Without consistent output/resource data, an operational system for a major department requires a year or more.

A related subject is permanency. Although the management team had confidence in each measure, measure 4 (LOC Productivity) initially did not accomplish its intended purpose of accurately combining project and enhancement LOC outputs. During the first year, deleted and changed LOC were not recorded; thus, the enhancement LOC was understated. After the automatic LOC counting system was enhanced, the measure became meaningful. Performance measures are subject to refinement and change, even when organizational functions remain constant.

Myth Three. All activities should be quantified.

After completing our performance ratios, the question was asked, "What percent of management's responsibilities are measured?" To answer the question, departmental responsibilities were grouped into three categories as noted in Figure 7.2. The first

FIGURE 7.2. Major responsibilities.

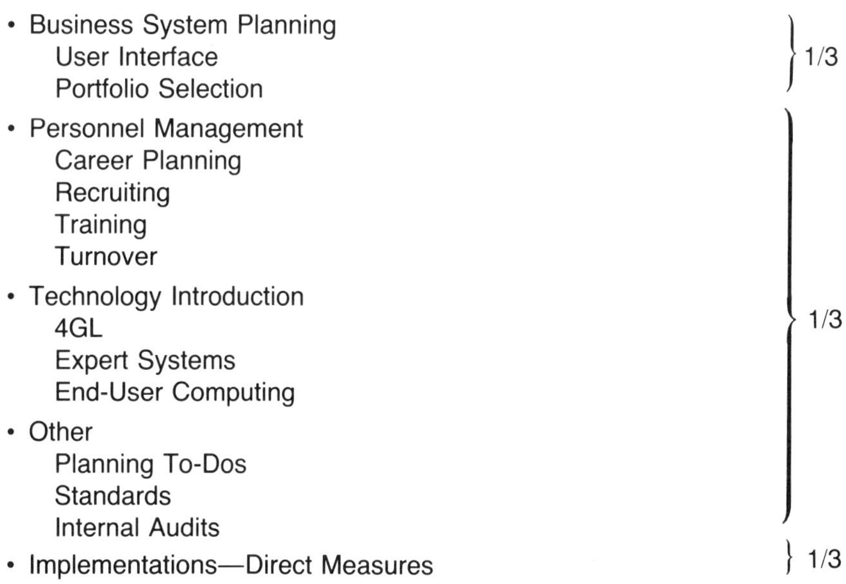

item, Business Systems Planning (BSP) was subjectively valued as one-third of our responsibilities. This involves selecting a portfolio of projects that optimize the corporate contribution. In other words, if a department is not working on the best projects for the company, productivity is a secondary factor.

The next third includes personnel management, introduction of technology, and other general management activities. The last third covers implementation activities. The nine performance measures defined are direct measures of this last activity. Business Systems Planning is not covered, and the middle third activities are only indirectly monitored by the performance measures. For example, if there is a strong training program, this should result in more productive project implementations and improved ratios.

Establishing performance measures for the other responsibilities is much more difficult because data is intangible and not repetitive. Projects, on the other hand, provide a base of comparison, especially when data on 10 or 15 projects is documented. Consider how difficult it would be to establish measures on the Business Systems Planning function. Who could provide a scale measuring the contribution of this planning activity?

In general, the value of purely quantitative measures depends on two variables: process structure and number of individual outputs. See Figure 7.3a for the software development activities. In the factory, the Implementation process, with high structure and volume, facilitated numeric performance measurement. However, the Design process lacks structure, as do other management activities where the value of quantitative measures is limited.

Activities in different functional areas of the corporation vary considerably in these factors. For example, the manufacturing process is inherently one of high structure and many outputs; a legal department might display low structure and possibly few major projects per year. Figure 7.3a and 7.3b links the two variables to functional areas, and also predicts the value of each combination. Since our direct experience only substantiates the software functions, other functional area placement in the matrix might be debated. Also, as with The Software Factory certain aspects of each functional area could be quantified with performance measurement.

FIGURE 7.3a. Software factory functions.

Process	MEASUREMENT VALUE: LOW	MEASUREMENT VALUE: HIGH
Structured	LOW Planning meeting Standards Audits	HIGH Project implementations Maintenance Info Center Service
Unstructured	VERY LOW Business Planning Career Planning Other Mgt. Activities	LOW System Design process
	FEW	MANY

NUMBER OF OUTPUTS

FIGURE 7.3b. Corporate functions.

Process	MEASUREMENT VALUE: LOW	MEASUREMENT VALUE: HIGH
Structured	LOW Engineering Finance	HIGH MIS Manufacturing Distribution
Unstructured	VERY LOW Personnel Legal	LOW Purchasing Marketing Product Management
	FEW	MANY

NUMBER OF OUTPUTS

Support versus development is also a distinction that must be made in most operating groups. There is usually some level of activity that goes to maintenance or support of existing facilities. Output versus resource should be separate for the support activity. Thus, for almost every group, there should be a minimum of two measures. This was not true for our Information Center, where only one measure was defined: Function Points divided by programming man-days. A dramatic increase obtained one year (10.2 vs. 6.8 Function Points per man-day) was due to cloning information requests and diverting resources from consulting/training activities, which were not measured, to the measured activity. Obviously, the second reason was not intended. Although the effort to define more measures can have a diminishing rate of return, in this case, consulting and training activities were monitored.

Myth Four. Department measures roll down.

All nine performance measures were established to measure department trends, the efforts of over 200 individuals. Assume the organizational hierarchy of programmer, Project Manager (6 to 12 staff), Systems Development Manager (25 to 30 staff), Director of Systems Development (200+ staff). Many people envision using performance measures at the first two levels, programmer and Project Manager. However, the value of our measures is in top-down order, with the majority of benefits at the Director level, some benefits at the Systems Development Manager and project levels, and minimal value at the individual level. To substantiate this point, consider the range of values reported by eight similar groups (Systems Development Manager level):

Measure	*Department Average*	*Range for Eight Systems Development Managers*
A. Productivity		
1. Support Productivity	173,400	115,700 to 311,600
2. Project Productivity	26,191	17,100 to 111,900
3. Function Point Productivity	.9	.47 to 2.21
B. Quality		
1. Maintenance UCRs	13,344	6,500 to 33,100
2. Project UCRs	8,182	2,900 to 39,800

Remember, these variances were in one organization with the same standards, productivity tools, experience level, and working environment. The difference among the groups is project uniqueness and application area; i.e., manufacturing, finance, order processing, marketing, distribution, purchasing, inventory control, and personnel.

The more groups in an average, the more reliable are the statistics. For example, department results were reasonably close to goals because the eight individual areas were averaged and the "law of large numbers" improved the reliability.

However, the lack of correlation to the department average does not necessarily imply lack of correlation from year-to-year of one particular group. With a few exceptions, based on unique projects, the variance for the same group from one year to the next was reasonable. Thus, establishing goals has value with staffs of 25 to 30 completing five to seven projects per year. At lower levels (smaller groups), project uniqueness produces inconsistencies.

Myth Five. Improvements automatically follow.

Some productivity experts recommend tracking ratios over time to establish trends. It was our philosophy that tracking was only part of the responsibility, along with setting objectives and defining how to improve—what tools and/or methodologies will positively impact the ratios. Over the years, an emphasis on productivity resulted in a variety of programming/testing software tools to perform functions, such as CRT screen generation, test data preparation, interactive program debug, and librarian functions. The maintenance environment utilizes these tools as well as restructuring code facilities.

Figure 7.4 lists ten approaches cross-referenced to the measures impacted. In our situation, the major items to pursue were the first three: monitor for consistent subsecond response time, formally implement the Joint Application Development (JAD) concept, and pursue COBOL code generators.

It may be surprising that fourth-generation languages (4GLs) are not on the list for consideration. After years of analysis, 4GLs are recommended exclusively for end-user "programming" of simple nonintegrated systems. Conversely, the Systems Develop-

FIGURE 7.4. How to improve.

Approach	*Performance Measures*								
	Productivity					*Qlty*		*Est*	
	1	*2*	*3*	*4*	*5*	*1*	*2*	*1*	*2*
1. Monitor for consistent subsecond response time	X	X	X	X	X			X	X
2. Implement the JAD design process		X	X	X					
3. Search for code generator	X	X	X	X	X	X	X	X	X
4. Continue to look for software application packages	X	X	X	X	X			X	X
5. Clone code		X	X	X	X				
6. Install faster terminals	X	X	X	X	X			X	X
7. Review the PC prototyping software		X	X	X					
8. Pursue improved testing tools						X	X		
9. Pursue estimating packages								X	X
10. Increase user system knowledge	X								

ment staff implements large, tailored, integrated complex corporate systems, not easily programmed or maintained with a 4GL.

Myth Six. Zero defects is the objective.

Attempting to maximize a productivity measure is not always logical since a balance of activities may produce a more optimal organizational result. For example, attempting to minimize support on systems could eventually produce an adverse effect, i.e., inability to support the system.

Consider the objective for Quality Measure Number 1, maintain or increase the Lines of Code per UCR. For some installations, improving operational quality might be the primary objective of the performance measurement program; however, our system operational quality was considered more than acceptable over the past few years. For example, in 1989, only one UCR occurred per year for every 13,344 LOC installed (not including project installations).

It may sound like poor management to admit an acceptable error level, and one might propose an absolute zero defects objective. However, if too much pressure is exerted by a ratio, negative ramifactions may result, such as delayed implementation dates because of unnecessary repetitive testing. Obviously, this logic is only appropriate when UCRs (program bugs) are under control. Also, the objectives must be attainable.

Other examples of not demanding 100 percent are illustrated by the two Estimating ratios; the goal is 80 percent. Is the objective too low, not demanding enough? Remember, when completing projects on time is the dominant goal, poor corporate decisions may result. For example, delaying known system enhancements may keep the project on schedule but cost significantly more to add after installation.

Myth Seven. Competing management methodologies are replaced.

The management process is generally defined as five activities: plan, organize, staff, direct, and control. Controlling involves monitoring results, usually through a reporting system. Our nine ratios are obviously directed at the control process, since we implemented the concept dealing strictly with numeric information. Other management methodologies, such as Critical Success Factors (CSF) or Management By Objective (MBO), primarily address the control function but are less quantitative than performance measures. They are more adaptable to planning, organizing, staffing, and directing activities.

Some would propose performance objectives as the primary tool; however, this is not recommended. Rather, performance measures should be used as an ancillary management tool.

Myth Eight. Corporate benefits are directly linked.

One surprising observation: Benefits to the corporation were not included in any of the calculations. By improving performance, there is an overall benefit to the company, but the value for individual projects is not input to the nine measures. Accumulating benefits for modern on-line systems is dependent on an organization's ability to quantify intangible contribution, a difficult task in a dynamic environment. However, if this is the objective, other approaches relying on management judgment are preferable to performance measurement.

Implementing a performance measurement methodology obviously requires resources and management attention. IBM states that 5 percent of the project budget should be directed toward measurement activities. In our case, almost all the work was accomplished via line management, those managers responsible for implementing the measures. If an organization is growing rapidly and involved in a number of new projects, it may not be an appropriate time to install a formal measurement program. For us, the basic factors such as Lines of Code, function points, and Unusual Condition Reports had been monitored for a number of years. Thus, the advantage was formalizing our approach and communicating it to everyone in the organization. Over time, this formal approach will help document productivity improvements.

Professor W. Skinner, author of "Productivity Paradox" (*Harvard Business Review*, July-August 1986) disclosed a potential disadvantage of productivity measures: "Managers under pressure to maximize productivity resist innovation". The objective must be to install the best overall corporate solution (application packages, end-user computing, 4GLs) versus maximizing ratios. The Function Point measures complement LOC measures, providing a balance and encouraging innovation.

CONCLUSION

Organizational and environmental factors dictate the value and type of measures. In our situation, a large number of projects provided stability in the ratios when all groups were included. Since most of the data needed were available, the cost of implementing performance measures was minimal; however, years were spent defining Function Points, collecting Unusual Condition Reports, and automating LOC data. The measures contributed to our organizational effectiveness and complement other management activities.

In retrospect, the process of implementing performance measures parallels other management tasks: define terms, set objectives, establish a plan, collect data, and monitor results. Line management should drive the process, although some staff support may be required. Simplicity in an operational program is important; if data collection is expensive or too many measures are defined, the benefits are diminished.

Managers must decide if their organizations are ready for performance measurement and, if so, how extensive a program is needed.

REFERENCES

Albrecht, A. J., and Gaffney, J. E., Jr. "Software Function, Source Lines of Code and Development Effort Predictions: A Software Science Validation." *IEEE Transactions on Software Engineering SE-9,* 6 (Nov. 1983), 639–648.

Skinner, W. "Productivity Paradox," *Harvard Business Review,* (July–Aug 1986).

CHAPTER 8

Quality and Japanese Just in Time Principles*

What is poor quality in software? It can be defined as unacceptable software performance; user dissatisfaction with an interface; missing or incorrect functions; many errors, program bugs and other implementation problems; or maintenance headaches.

This chapter focuses on what is called "operational quality," or sometimes "technical quality," as opposed to functional quality. In line with this, responsiblity for quality is assigned to the software developers themselves and not a separate quality assurance (QA) department. This approach is identified with certain Japanese just-in-time (JIT) manufacturing techniques, including line management control, correcting one's own errors, continuous error detection and easy-to-see quality. (Ref Fig. 8.1)

LESSON FROM JAPAN

A major emphasis of the Japanese just-in-time (JIT) manufacturing philosophy is quality. In applying JIT principles to qual-

*Adapted from Johnson, James R. "Hallmark's Formula for Quality". *Datamation* (Feb. 15, 1990), pp 119–122.

FIGURE 8.1 How JIT principles can improve software quality.

A number of principles used for many years in manufacturing operations can be adapted to improve the production of software.

JIT Principle	Purpose	IS Impact and Techniques
1. Line management control (versus quality assurance department)	Motivation	Granting project team responsibility
2. Correcting one's errors	Learning	Granting project team responsibility
3. Continuous error detection	Removing errors	Test plans Development methodology CASE
4. Easy-to-see quality	Measuring	Known metrics (of production problems) Post implementation audit

ity control in software development, it is important to ask how similar is manufacturing to software development.

JIT contains at least four concepts that can be applied to software development: line management control, correcting one's own errors, continuous error detection and easy-to-see quality.

Line management control, which can be controversial, places primary responsibility for quality with line management rather than with a separate quality control department. In such an arrangement, what had been the QC department becomes a facilitator, says Richard Schonberger in his book *Japanese Manufacturing Techniques: Nine Hidden Lessons in Simplicity*.

"The QC department, much reduced in size, promotes the removal of defect causes, keeps track of quality accomplishments, monitors operations to see that standard procedures are followed . . . and coordinates QC training. . . . Line management has the primary responsiblity for quality, and foremen should be the quality experts," writes Schonberger.

Applying the principle of line management control in IS means the project manager has responsiblity for quality from design through implementation.

The principle of correcting one's own errors refers to rework—insisting that software developers correct errors found in testing or after installation. Learning from mistakes is an effective training technique. Implementing the principle is an organizational issue—the software development team must be responsible for correcting errors during design and testing, although other groups may be involved.

Continuous error detection means checking quality while the work is in progress. Design inspections, code walk-throughs and unit testing are all techniques to use to improve quality during the production process. Establishing procedures (a methodology) and intermediate quality milestones help enforce process control.

The Japanese implement easy-to-see quality with visual graphics. "Display boards are everywhere in Japanese plants. They tell the worker, bosses, customers and outside visitors what quality factors are measured, what the recent performance is, what the current quality improvement projects are, who has won awards for quality, and so forth," Schonberger writes. "Some displays are lighted electronic devices resembling basketball scoreboards which call for help when there are quality problems."

In MIS, the electronic scoreboard would obviously be extreme; documenting quality metrics for each project is more reasonable.

Line Management/Correcting Errors

In the software factory, the project team is responsible for quality control; a separate quality organization does not exist. Also, the developers have post-implementation responsibility: maintenance is not transferred to a separate group immediately after implementation.

Years ago, after one particularly poor implementation, creating a separate QA organization was considered. However, improved testing procedures, created by the project group concerned, solved the implementation problem. The end users, who were not satisfied with the quality of the system either, agreed that the proposed testing methods, which included creating a duplicate system for parallel testing, were adequate. Subsequent results have proven them correct.

This is not to imply that every MIS organization should forego establishing a separate QA department, of course. The advantage of having an outsider check the less obvious and less frequently used features of a system has merit. Also, an organization with an inexperienced staff or with obsolete, antiquated methodologies may not have a successful track record. Thus, having an independent group test the software is a safe way to improve the product. But if an experienced staff organization has proven methods and a series of successes, then giving that staff complete responsibility for quality is a motivating factor. And the principle of allowing line management to be in control will work.

Continuous Error Detection

The success and quality of a project implementation is directly related to the quality of the system test plan. For critical projects, a formal written plan is a requirement. For less critical projects, an informal written plan is employed. The organization has defined four primary testing levels: unit, integration, system and user acceptance. The formal written test plan encompasses the last three levels. The following definitions explain these primary tests:

- **Unit.** Testing of all logic paths in the programs with generated (test) or production data to ensure correctness of individual programs.
- **Integration.** Coordinated testing of multiple programs with generated or production data. The purpose is to ensure correctness of individual programs.
- **System.** Execution of the system in a production-like environment to ensure that the system operates properly from both program and procedural stand-points.
- **User Acceptance.** User's participation in planning and testing,

as well as in inputting test data and reviewing the results. Ensures that the user understands the system's operational requirements, capabilities and deliverables. The user acceptance test may be part of the system test.

Other test plans, such as disaster recovery or volume tests, are performed as needed. (Reference Chapter 16.)

The written test plan includes an overview, a test plan procedure, test plan details, conversion plan and an appendix. The level of detail in the testing required by the plan may vary considerably from one system to another. For each primary testing level, the plan should call for testing divided into cycles, such as daily cycle, a weekly cycle, a monthly cycle, etc. Each cycle is then divided into steps made up of setting up test cases and predictions of expected results. Including the name of the individual assigned to specific tests may also be appropriate. Details of the conditions to be tested for each step are usually placed in the appendix.

Who teaches the staff how to write a good test plan? The approach was to circulate the best written plans to all project groups. Thus, incremental improvements in writing test plans and in the testing itself occurred over the years.

Using a computer-aided software engineering methodology, which automates structured design and programming activities, can obviously also improve quality. But even for those companies that have both the upper CASE analysis and design tools and the lower CASE code generator systems in operation, a written system test plan is a useful complement to the CASE tools.

Easy-to-see Quality

To determine quality, measurements and reports must exist. A recommended approach is to use a problem management system linked to quality measures and a post implementation procedure to analyze projects. Under the problem management system, all technical problems (programming, procedural, data, hardware, etc.) are documented in an Unusual Condition Report (UCR). Each UCR represents and records a single problem.

For example, the UCRs for all systems installed during 1989 were recorded for an arbitrary three-month period following their installation. After the three-month period, each system is considered to be in maintenance. As expected, more errors occurred during the installation period than in maintenance.

Technical quality is computed using a quantitative formula: the number of lines of code (LOC) in a system divided by the number of UCRs issued for that system, yielding a ratio. The higher the ratio, the higher the quality of the product.

Figure 8.2, "Quality Measurements," shows the combined ratio for all of the 1989 projects. The ratio reflects the operational quality of the systems produced and the thoroughness of project installation planning. This measure does not measure user functionality or how the system contributes to the goals of the corporation, however. Is the ratio fair? The denominator, number of UCRs, is an independently recorded factor for all projects. But what if the numerator, LOC, is inflated? Each organization must verify the validity of its LOC statistics. Still, extreme emphasis can result in negative ramifications. This formula is used primarily as an internal measure of project performance. No single quality measure is used independent of anything else. (Reference Chapter 7.)

The objective in 1989 was for all systems was to exceed 7,500 LOC per UCR. Three projects, ranging in size from 319 to 1,044 man-days, are listed in Figure 8.3 entitled "How Three Projects Fared." Since the quality ratios vary dramatically (5,360 to 59,400) among projects, is it a reasonable measure? By itself, without amplifying information, probably not. Those viewing the results might ask, How critical were the errors? Did external dates force an abbreviated test? Was extensive parallel testing possible? Were antiquated systems changed? However, from a technical standpoint, all things being equal, the project manager of project C produced a very high-quality system, seven times the 7,500 LOC/UCR objective.

Monitoring UCRs in the maintenance stage is the objective of a second quality ratio measurement. This figure measures the general operational quality of a system after installation. The maintenance measure concentrates on the support function, which includes production fixes and enhancements that take less than 75 man-days. (Enhancements that take longer than 75 man-days would be defined as a separate project.) Only UCRs caused by the

Systems Development Department are counted. Other problems are excluded.

For some installations, improving operational quality might be the primary objective of the performance measurement program. However, our operational quality has been considered to be more than acceptable over the past few years. For example, in 1989 only one UCR was issued for every 13,344 LOC installed. The general objective was to hold steady or increase above the 11,000 level for the maintenance quality measure.

Post implementation audits provide a database to assess quality. About half of the projects completed receive an audit by internal personnel (those employed by the software factory versus external auditors). Some typical questions for performing a post-implementation audit are:

- How well has the installed system performed in the production environment?
- Was the system easy to use?
- Were the users satisfied with the system's capabilities?
- How many enhancements have been requested?
- Has Systems Development been able to support the system easily?
- Has the Data Center been able to meet the production schedule?
- How many UCRs were written during the first three months after installation?

For example, one recent system has performed very well in production; only three UCRs were written during the first three months after installation. The users find the system easy to use and are satisfied with its capabilities. The minor enhancements requested have been installed in less than five man-days. (Reference Chapter 17.)

Although many companies use conventional quality control departments successfully, our approach links Japanese manufacturing principles to the software development and maintenance process (motivation, learning, removing errors and measuring). By assigning responsibility for quality directly to project managers, line management becomes responsible for correcting errors and

FIGURE 8.2 Quality measurements.

The first equation shows Hallmark's quality ratio for all projects installed in 1989. The objective was to exceed 8,000 LOC per UCR. The second equation shows the quality of maintenance for 1989.

Quality Measure 1 (Averages for all projects)

$$\frac{2{,}610{,}000 \text{ (Lines of Code)}}{319 \text{ (Number of UCRs)}} = 8{,}182 \text{ (Project UCR Ratio)}$$

	1986	1987	1988	1989
Four-Year Project UCR Ratio	5,530	7,984	8,938	8,182

Quality Measure 2 (Averages for all projects)

$$\frac{17{,}200{,}000 \text{ (Lines of Code)}}{1{,}289 \text{ (Nonproject UCRs)}} = 13{,}344 \text{ (Maintenance UCR Ratio)}$$

FIGURE 8.3. How three projects fared.

Projects A and B did not meet the 7,500 UCR ratio goal; project C soared past it.

QUALITY VS. PROJECT SIZE

	A	B	C
1. Man-Days	319	978	1,044
2. New LOC	16,800	53,800	118,400
3. Changed LOC	10,000	10,900	400
4. Total LOC	26,800	64,700	118,400
5. Function Points	131	634	463
6. UCRs	5	16	2
7. Project UCR Ratio (quality)	5,360	4,044	59,400

for final system quality. A thorough testing procedure specified by a written plan for system and acceptance tests assures continuous error detection. Production problem metrics and post-implementation audits promote easy-to-see quality. This approach many not apply to every organization, but it does work.

REFERENCES

Schonberger, Richard J., *Japanese Manufacturing Techniques: Nine Hidden Lessons in Simplicity* (New York: The Free Press 1982).

PART IV

Motivation

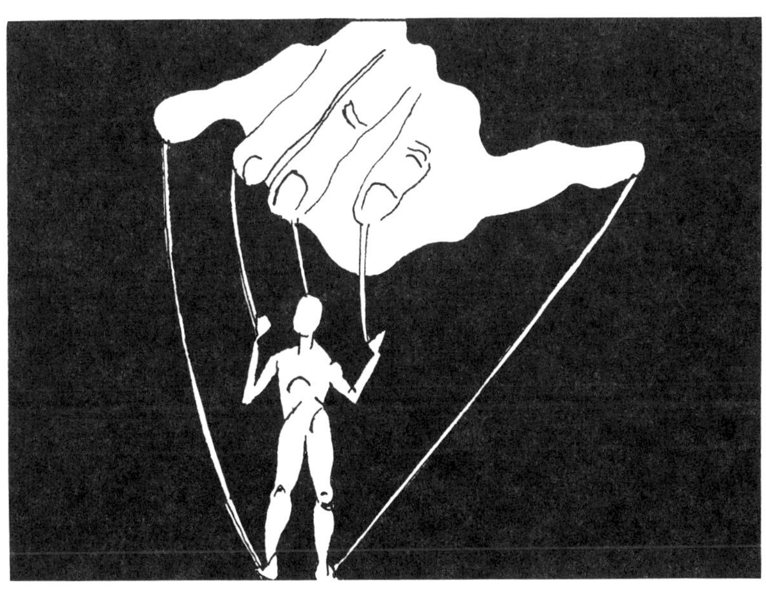

This part on personnel management does not provide a comprehensive treatment. Rather, it is focused on two topics: performance reviews and job rotation.

In our company, performance reviews are formal sessions between a manager and employee conducted in January each year. A standard form is provided. The ratings on the review are linked to salary increases via the Hay system, a salary administration technique followed by many corporations. In Chapter 9, the review techniques developed over the years in the Software Factory are explained as well as other options.

Job enrichment and career planning discussions (chap. 10) are covered mid-year, using an internal resume (a tailored form) as the focus. This is also a formal, private meeting, but has a completely different purpose than the performance review. Career planning is the process of rotating employees to different application areas, providing a wide range of experience needed for promotion, and fighting complacency, a "burnout" that develops when individuals stay on the same job too long.

One of the best articles about motivation is the Harvard Business Review classic "One More Time: How Do You Motivate Employees?" by Frederick Herzberg (initially published in 1968, republished in 1987). To quote:

> *Money, benefits, comfort, and so on are "hygiene" factors—they create dissatisfaction if they're absent, but they don't make people feel good about their jobs and give them the needed internal generator. What does produce the generator are recognition of achievement, pride in doing a good job, more responsibility, advancement, and personal growth. The secret is job enrichment.*

Providing job enrichment in a Software Factory is a difficult task. From an organizational perspective, specialization and separation of duties are barriers to individual recognition, achievement, and responsibility. Consider the departments created in many factories:

Area	*Function*
Quality Control	Assure workers don't install error-prone systems.
Auditing	Monitor employees for correct standards and controls.
Pseudo-Users	Interface between DP and end user (customer).
Database	Separate group to define customer data needs.
Information Center	Solve customer for immediate needs.

Obviously, environmental factors control key organizational decisions that are long-term issues. However, if employee motivation is a priority, careful consideration must be given to reporting relationships and department responsibilities. One of the most basic decisions is the separation of the system design and programming functions. Our approach for the past 10 years has been a combined position of Programmer/Analyst. In addition, we assume quality control is each project team's responsibility, encourage direct contact between customers and the programming/design team, utilize database as a support function rather than driver, and rotate staff through the Information Center. Referencing Herzberg's terms, all these activities allow for vertical job loading, more responsibility, and growth.

Another aspect of motivation is personal recognition by management and peers. Management classes generally focus on human relations or sensitivity training. If the course is worthwhile, the lesson equates to both commonsense and the golden rule: Treat others as you would like them to treat you.

CHAPTER 9

Performance Reviews

Consider the following performance review process:

The manager discusses annual performance with employee. A rating indicating performance is included. The review form is subsequently signed and placed in the employee's personnel file.

Defining the goals of the performance review process is a controversial task; for example, which of the following objectives should be included? Write Yes or No by each item.

Purpose of Performance Review
1. Motivation
2. Communicate priorities
3. Quantity expected outputs (numerically)
4. Career planning
5. Review past year's objectives
6. Establish a monthly plan for next year
7. Improve employee's self-esteem
8. Document performance

9. Establish promotability
10. Document accomplishments
11. Thank employee
12. Document personal traits (strengths/weaknesses)
13. Justify rating
14. Explain salary increase
15. Improve current job
16. Provide rating

Our approach results in nine Nos and only seven Yeses. As Figure 9.1 illustrates, objectives not considered are part of the continuous management process, the day-to-day responsibilities of management, or other separate activities, such as, career planning, job enrichment, promotion-planning, and salary administration. Each company may select different performance review objectives, but having too many is not recommended.

Assuming agreement on the objectives, does the performance review form include a section for each objective? Ours has six sections:

	Section	*Objective*
One	Assignment (tasks and last year's objectives)	Review last year's objectives (5) Document accomplishments (10)
Two	Performance/contribution	Document performance (8) Justify rating (13)
Three	Rating	Provide rating (16)
Four	Assignment/objectives/ priorities for next year	Communicate priorities (2)
Five	Traits—both strengths and weaknesses	Document traits influencing performance (12)
Six	Comments or notable discussion items	

Comments on each section follow in sequence. For selected sections, both a recommendation and alternative are included.

FIGURE 9.1. Purpose of performance reviews.

NO	YES
Continuous Mgt. Process	**Annual Perf. Review**
1. Motivation	2. Communicate Priorities
3. Quantify Outputs	5. Review Past Year's Objectives
6. Monthly Plan	8. Document Performance
7. Improve Employee Self-Esteem	10. Document Accomplishments
11. Thank Employee	12. Document Traits (Strengths and Weaknesses) Impacting Performance
	13. Justify Rating
	16. Provide Rating
Separate	
4. Career Planning	
9. Establish Promotability	
14. Explain Salary Increase	
15. Improve Current Job	
9	7

SECTION ONE—ASSIGNMENT (TASKS AND LAST YEAR'S OBJECTIVES)

Recommended: Define specifically what tasks the individual was assigned. Include specific objectives from last year's review (section four). For most MIS environments, a time-reporting or project management system provides documentation. If an automated system is not used, monthly status reports or employee input is recommended. The example is for Dean, a manager:

- *Managed a staff of 30 professionals via three project managers.*
- *Group was responsible for the order processing system, an application critical to the corporation.*
- *Seven significant enhancements totalling over 3,000 man-days were installed, including project XYZ (1,600 man-days).*
- *275 minor enhancements accounted for 1,100 man-days.*
- *Interfacing with the production committee is an important part of the position.*
- *General objectives for the year were: developing people, meeting schedules, controlling program errors, motivating staff, interfacing with other divisions, contributing on high-level design issues, reviewing system test plans, and justifying business systems.*
- *Performed the general management functions required of the position: organize, plan, motivate, monitor.*

Alternative: Restate the job description. This is not recommended because a generalized job description does not explain specific responsibilities. For example:

- *Directs the work of Programmers, Programmer/Analysts, and Senior Programmer/Analysts via Systems Development Project Managers.*
- *Reviews user requests to determine the feasibility or practicality of a project.*
- *Schedules and assigns projects to effectively utilize programming resources.*
- *Monitors the status of projects to assure that completion dates are met.*
- *Communicates status of new projects to user groups to assist in the implementation of new systems.*
- *Maintains communication upwards and downwards to assure data processing objectives are understood.*

SECTION TWO—PERFORMANCE/CONTRIBUTION

Recommended: Performance/Contribution is the most important section. It justifies the rating by documenting how well the individual completed or executed the responsibilities defined in section one. Both positive and negative comments are included. The example references the recommended assignment above.

To manage the order processing groups successfully, one must concentrate on end-user interfaces and control-production errors. In his role as production committee member, Dean exceeded expectations by communicating effectively and proposing new ideas. He had extensive involvement in critical design issues, for example, direct participation in the Verification project and the Incentive program. This involvement assured a pragmatic design and is an important contribution.

Addressing production errors on existing systems, no major problems occurred during the year, but the number of program errors, although controlled, was higher than last year. Part of the increase was due to the seven major implementations.

The largest project implemented was the XYZ system, requiring over 1,600 man-days. It was completed close to schedule and considered a success by both MIS and the user department. The installed system will reduce operating cost and improve service to the customer. From an MIS technical point of view, the program errors were higher than expected. This is partially due to the new technology used, but more thorough testing was possible. When a run-time problem surfaced, the team immediately responded with design changes to correct the situation. Other major implementations were successfully installed on schedule.

Individual accomplishments were significant. The three most noteworthy were: (1) presenting our prototyping approach at a national conference, (2) completing the Workbench study, a well-written logical document substantiating our current approach to programmer productivity, and (3) reducing the production system run-time by one and one-half hours.

On general management issues, Dean deserves credit for developing individuals so they can assume more responsibility and for motivating the group by showing interest in their work and careers.

Alternative: The easiest way to write a nebulous review is to emphasize personal traits (communication, cooperation, attitude, creativity, decisiveness, dependability, thoroughness, etc.) which were not directly relevant to job performance. Justifying the rating with flowery terms and adjectives is the second common mistake. An extreme example of a poor performance/contribution section follows:

Dean is an energetic, conscientious and versatile employee. He is studious by nature, has an excellent education, and is extremely accurate and thor-

ough in his work. He has an alert, active mind, and quickly perceives and correctly evaluates the essential elements of any problem, and arrives at a sound solution. Tactful and diplomatic, he has the ability to express and strongly support his views on controversial subjects without arousing antagonism or resentment. He speaks and writes with great clarity, and, accordingly, is outstanding as an instructor. Dignified, of excellent appearance, he has a personality and personal characteristics that inspire confidence. Likeable, with an excellent sense of humor and an ingrained respect for his fellow man, he secures a high degree of loyalty and cooperation from his subordinates, in whom he instills a rare sense of personal responsibility for the quality of their work. Dean is a leader in every respect and is thoroughly well-qualified to assume greater responsibilities.

Does this description say anything about what the person did or his contribution to the organization? This alternative is not recommended.

Another issue is whether or not to solicit an employee's self-evaluation: Should the employee prepare section two? Although some suggest this approach, most agree it may lead to confrontation, and it is therefore avoided. However, it is helpful to request the employee's input to ensure important activities are not overlooked. The manager (Dean) might provide information on his activities: major individual accomplishments; special studies completed with comment on personal involvement and importance; role in significant implementations or support; i.e., credit deserved for staff accomplishments; and efforts that could have been better.

SECTION THREE—RATING

Recommended/Alternatives: This section is the most controversial and, since the correct approach depends on the corporate environment, there is more than one "right" answer. The discussion is divided into five areas addressing the following questions:

a. Does a performance curve exist? (Yes, No)

b. What is the distribution of the curve? (average, above average)

c. What controls the curve? (guidelines, budget)

d. What rating technique is used? (subjective, objective, relative)

e. What are the performance titles? (good, average, meets expectations)

Recommendations are included with the discussion of each question.

a. The primary question is: Does a performance curve exist, and, if so, how many exceed the norm? Arguments for no rating contradict our competitive nature—everyone keeps score in sports and school from grade school through college. The pass/fail grading system introduced 15 years ago for selected college courses exists, but has lost popularity. Thus, we will assume individuals should be placed on a performance curve, although stronger arguments could be made for the pass/fail system in business.

b. Curve distribution is the next question. How many categories should exist, should 5 percent be in the top category or 30 percent or 75 percent? Answers depend on corporate tradition, but consider the following options:

Guideline Percents

Rank	*A*	*B*	*C*	*D*	*E*
1	5%	30%	5%	75%	
2	35%	30%	55%	20%	
3	60%	40%	40%	5%	None
4	0–5%	0–5%	0–5%	0–5%	

The recommendation is option C, having the majority of staff receive an "above average" rating. Options A and B create problems since the majority of staff are considered average, a definite disappointment. Option D is unrealistic, either the staff is overqualified or the expectations are too low.

Related to distribution is the issue of position hierarchy. Should the distribution apply to each management level? For example, if there are 10 project managers, 10 senior analysts, and 10 programmer/analysts, do the guidelines apply to each level? Philosophically, the answer may be Yes, but, in reality, some rationalize that a manager was promoted based on performance and thus should not be given an "average" rating.

c. Assuming guideline percentages are applied, some controls must exist or "rating inflation" results. The usual control is linking the ratings to the budget via salary increases or simply enforcing the percentages by area. The military rating system illustrates the consequences of no control. Performance ratings influence promotion but have no influence on budget. Also, since the rater is not limited by percents, the majority of people are placed in the top 1 percent or 5 percent category.

d. Subjective, objective, and relative are the three possible rating methods. Subjective is based on management's judgment. Objective rating requires specific goals or performance criteria, such as, install XYZ system by June 15 or stay within 5 percent of the budget. With the relative method, performance rank is determined by comparing those performing similar functions. In practice, a combination of all three is generally employed. Obviously, if only one person is independently rated, the relative technique has no meaning. The advisability of a strictly objective numerical rating system is discussed in section 4.

e. Related to ratings are performance titles. Consider the following options:

Rank	*A*	*B*	*C*	*D*
1	Outstanding	Excellent	Far exceeds expectations	Stands out from all others
2	Very good	Above average	Consistently exceeds	Superior to most
3	Good	Average	Meets expectations	Exceeds job requirements
4	Poor	Fair	Below expectations	Unsatisfactory

One might ask, does it really matter? True, the issue is less important than the rating technique and may not be a major concern, but the wording in either columns A or C is preferred over B and D. Also, C has an additional advantage of focusing on expectations of a particular position.

SECTION FOUR—ASSIGNMENT/OBJECTIVES/ PRIORITIES

Recommended: Document next year's assignment to the extent known. State general objectives the individual can control, and document specific priorities. For example, a manager's section four:

Concentrate on the following

Developing people
Meeting schedules
Reducing UCRs
Motivating staff
Interfacing with other divisions
Contributing on high-level design issues
Reviewing system test plans
Justifying business systems
Completing department special objectives, to-do's, and individual assignments
One specific priority is the code generator study with a December completion date.

Alternative: Defining specific quantified results, mostly numeric, is an option possible for certain positions. The concept proposes that manager and employee agree to goals and develop "yardsticks" to measure superior performance.

In most professional areas, setting specific objectives at the beginning of the year is not possible because tasks beyond one and two months in the future are not known. Also, setting quality or quantity measures on vague or unknown tasks is impossible. In some areas where people are on production quotas, such as six "outputs" per day with a 20 percent acceptance ratio, the objective-setting process can work very well. But in most professional areas such as Finance, Product Management, and the Software Factory, defining specific objectives early in the year is not possible.

SECTION FIVE—STRENGTHS AND WEAKNESSES

The section on strengths and weaknesses is the place to document individual traits, some that may not have been included in section two. A worksheet with common skills or traits provides thought-starters, although this section is relatively easy to complete. A brief set of traits or skills are:

Work Related	*People and Leadership*	*Effectiveness*
Quantity of Work	Leadership	Innovation
Quality of Work	Delegation	Ambition/

Work Related	*People and Leadership*	*Effectiveness*
Design Ability	Planning	Aggressiveness
Thoroughness	Communications—Verbal and Written	Dependability/Dedication
Organization	Cooperation Working within Relationship—MIS	Tenacity—Follow-Through
Effort	Cooperation with User	Decisiveness
Technical Ability		Initiative—Self-Motivation
Neatness/Accuracy		Creativity
Ability to Meet Target Dates		Attitude
		Commonsense
		Proper Allocation of Time
		Works to Full Potential

For example:

Extensive MIS Expertise—Thorough knowledge of management aspects of MIS.

Corporate Knowledge—Relates well to business areas as demonstrated on Project XYZ.

Decisive—Decision-making is strength, as noted on productivity study.

Motivation/Leadership—Able to motivate staff. Group has high productivity and morale.

Organization Ability—Did an outstanding job on department organization study.

Communication—Professional presenter as demonstrated on department presentation and other updates to management.

Analysis—Logical and intelligent approach to problems, specifically noted on Project UVW.

Business Knowledge—Understands business opportunities thoroughly, for example, memo on scanner technology.

Note that specific examples are included, some repeated from section 2.

SECTION SIX—COMMENTS

The Comments section is used for items brought up during the discussion by either individual, which are not recorded elsewhere in this document. Also, for specific plans, projects, programs, etc. for improving employee's performance. Example:

Attend a state-of-the-art seminar for professional growth.
Dean is interested in a technical management position, such as database.

OTHER APPROACHES

The perspective on performance reviews is from a large company with a structured approach. Other approaches or new ideas:

Rating groups versus individuals,
Individual writing their own review, and
Peer ratings versus manager's ratings.

The issue of how, and when, to "rate" performance will be debated for years. For opposing views note the references below (Gellerman versus Roger). The organizational environment also plays an important role. For example, if reviews are confidential, relative ratings can work; however, if not, a less structured approach is recommended.

REFERENCES

Gellerman, Saul W. and Hodgson, William G., "Cyanamid's New Take on Performance Appraisal", Harvard Business Review, (May–June, 1988), P. 36.

Herzberg, Frederick. "One More Time: How Do You Motivate Employees?" *Harvard Business Review,* (Sept.–Oct. 1987).

Roger T. J., "No Excuses Management," Harvard Business Review, (July–August, 1990), 84

CHAPTER 10

Job Rotation

HISTORY

Early in 1974, three 10-man-year projects were implemented. As support activities replaced development work, project member motivation deteriorated and team productivity suffered. The support staffing consisted of the programming team that developed each project. In an attempt to create more interesting jobs, the managers decided to rotate half of each project team to a different support system, one they had not developed. This was a risky action since individuals were not requesting reassignment and system experience would be dramatically reduced.

The result surprised everyone. Rotated individuals quickly learned their new systems and brought fresh ideas and enthusiasm to the team. A minor, but potentially major, morale problem no longer existed; project members were excited about their jobs.

PHILOSOPHY

Were the circumstances unique in this situation, since a letdown is always possible after project implementation? Our experience indicated that anyone can become complacent in a job after development of the project in support. Thus, the "burnout" theory:

> *After 2 to 4 years in a position, productivity peaks, performance drops off, and complacency or boredom may result. The best way to improve productivity, assuming a promotion is not available, is a lateral rotation to a different system.*

Based on this theory, staff rotations have occurred every year since 1974. During the past four years, the rotation statistics are as follows:

		Number of Job Rotations				
	Total Staff	*All Nonmgmt. Positions*	*First-Line Mgrs.*	*Second-Line Mgrs.*	*Total*	*%*
1985	231	40	5	4	49	21
1986	232	30	7	0	37	16
1987	238	37	7	4	46	19
1988	238	32	6	1	39	16

The numbers do not include changes resulting from promotions. Rotations all occur during February each year, corresponding with the annual staffing of new projects. Thus, a Software Factory provides a natural environment for rotation as projects are completed and others started.

Since not all projects complete at year end, other rotations take place during the year involving another 5 percent of the staff. Thus, approximately 25 percent of the staff is rotated in a given year. After allowing for turnover, this results in an average rotation period of between 3 to 3.5 years.

Note the statistics include both first- and second-line managers. Obviously, careful planning is required to assure adequate continuity and system knowledge for a given system, but the theory applies to all positions.

PREREQUISITES

A few years ago, I explained the rotation policy to a manager of a comparable programming staff. Since his total lack of interest on the subject was puzzling, I asked why he didn't believe in the concept. He replied, "The theory is sound, but my organization has 25 percent turnover and no base of experience; thus, rotation doesn't apply. Rather, my challenge is to maintain all knowledge on the project team."

This is obviously a good point and limits the execution of a rotation plan. Thus, the first prerequisite: The organization must have stability; high turnover (over 15 to 20 percent) or significant staff expansion limit the practicality of the policy. The number of rotations in our environment may not be appropriate for other organizations; however, a few strategic rotations would apply in most environments.

The second prerequisite is top management participation. This is necessary for two reasons. First, since staff is rotated among managers, each manager has a personal interest in obtaining the best employees and, conversely, rotating out of their group average performers. The manager of the managers must participate to ensure that talent and experience are balanced, or, if imbalanced, distributed to accomplish the objectives of the organization. Secondly, top management has to interface with user managers who uniformly argue not to rotate staff supporting their areas. This attitude is expected since relationships have been established and there is a fear that rotated staff will have a long learning curve. Arguments (rotation benefits) to placate these concerns are the personal and organizational benefits of job rotation.

PERSONAL BENEFITS

Job interest is dramatically increased. Required learning creates challenges, improves motivation, and fights complacency. A new productivity curve is started, one that will exceed the previous curve. Also, working with a new manager and team provides those rotated with a fresh start, analogous to starting a new job with another corporation. Have you ever contemplated what you might do differently starting your job over?

ORGANIZATION BENEFITS

The primary organizational benefit is improved productivity resulting from a challenged, experienced staff. The learning curve is surprisingly short. Thus, the immediate loss in productivity is offset in six to nine months.

Job rotation dispels systems mysticism by eliminating positions of unique expertise where only one individual, the mystic, can answer questions. Because mystics rarely document their knowledge, they become bottlenecks to the organization, controlling the information to maintain a position of power. With an active rotation policy, there is no place for the protective mystic attitude. Rather, rotated individuals take pride in leaving a well-documented system.

JOB ROTATION EXECUTION

Executing the rotation policy in our environment directly involves eight managers, who are each responsible for 30 staff members, including 3 to 5 project managers, and the overall manager. All 200+ staff members report to this management group of nine. The process is explained by a series of steps:

1. Each manager is asked to identify rotation candidates based on time in position. Those with two or more years on the same project are listed, with the longest time in position at the top.
2. The list is refined based on constraints. For example, if a project is in the implementation phase scheduled for a June date, no rotations may be planned for February. Also, if a project is supported by two people, it is illogical to rotate both at the same time.
3. The internal resume form, completed at mid-year, documents individual preferences. The form (Figure 11.1) has three sections relating to job rotation: work interests and activities, areas of interest, and job preferences/objectives. Typical requests might be: on-line programming, a large project assignment, database design, or a different functional area. This information is referenced in Step 5.
4. Next, a combined list of all open positions, both for new projects and those created by rotations, is published for the management team. A brief description of position responsibilities is included if not obvious.
5. In a series of three or four meetings, the managers match the open positions with the candidates. It is an iterative process

where the optimal solution is pursued, a solution not necessarily satisfying every department and personal goal, but satisfying as many as possible. If more information is needed from individuals to clarify their interests, managers will discuss possible positions with them. After the plan stabilizes, one change may cause a chain reaction; for this reason, the rotations are not considered optional. Only in rare cases have the managers misinterpreted individual desires. When this happens, alternatives are pursued.

Management could be criticized for not involving the staff directly in the rotation planning. But it is not practical to post jobs and conduct "interviews" when so many changes take place. Conversely, as openings occur during the year, interviews are possible for many positions.

6. Communicating the changes to all those involved is done expeditiously. All physical moves are planned within two weeks on the same day. Communication to other personnel and managers occurs as appropriate.

LEAVING THE SOFTWARE FACTORY

As shown in Fig. 10.1, questions are also asked about interests outside of the Software Factory, both within MIS or in a user-functional area. Our role in these job changes is as facilitator, not planner. As positions are announced, we circulate the announcements to the entire staff. Thus, our staff must first express an interest in an outside position before interviews are arranged. Of course, exceptions do occur when someone is selected for a position, but, in general, the "raiding" philosophy for lateral positions is discouraged.

WORK INTERESTS AND ACTIVITIES

In the first column, show the degree of interest you have in the activity listed. In the second column, show how much each activity exists in your current job. Scale your rating from a low of 0 to a high of 5. In the third column, asterisk three activities most important to you.

FIGURE 10.1. Internal resume form.

A. Activities

	Interest	*Curr. Job*	*Most Imp.*
1. Large Projects (over 75 MD)	—	—	—
	—	—	—
2. Small Projects (under 75 MD)	—	—	—
3. Support	—	—	—
4. Programming	—	—	—
5. Design			
6. CICS	—	—	—
7. SUPRA (Database)	—	—	—
8. Personal Computers	—	—	—
9. System 38/RPG III	—	—	—
10. MARK IV/FOCUS	—	—	—
11. Train/Lead/Interface with Team/Users	—	—	—
12. Work Alone	—	—	—
13. Plan/Estimate/Present Projects	—	—	—
14. Other ______________	—	—	—

Work Interests and Activities

In the first column, show the degree of interest you have in the activity listed. In the second column, show how much each activity exists in your current job. Scale your rating from a low of 0 to a high of 5. In the third column, asterisk three activities most important to you.

FIGURE 10.1. Continued

B. Areas of Interest (check interest level—optional as appropriate)

Inside Systems Development

	LOW	*MED*	*HIGH*
1. Marketing	—	—	—
2. Order Processing	—	—	—
3. Distribution	—	—	—
4. Inventory Management	—	—	—
5. Mfg./Materials	—	—	—
6. Pre-Production	—	—	—
7. Finance	—	—	—
8. EI/Personnel	—	—	—
9. Fixtures	—	—	—
10. Info Center	—	—	—
11. Creative ("CARDS")	—	—	—
12. Technology	—	—	—
13. Productivity Coord.	—	—	—
14. Standards Analyst	—	—	—
15. Other ____________	—	—	—

Outside Systems Development

	LOW	*MED*	*HIGH*
1. Database Admin.	—	—	—
2. MIS Training	—	—	—
3. End-User Technology	—	—	—
4. Data Communications	—	—	—
5. Network Support	—	—	—
6. Operating Systems	—	—	—
7. Technical Support	—	—	—
8. Computer Res. Mgmt.	—	—	—
9. Prod. Mgmt. Services	—	—	—
10. Marketing	—	—	—
11. Finance	—	—	—
12. Internal Audit	—	—	—
13. Matls Mgmt./Purchasing	—	—	—
14. Operations Research	—	—	—
15. Other ____________	—	—	—

FIGURE 10.1. Continued

C. Objective/Job Preferences

A. Comments on present responsibilities—(what liked most, least):

B. I would like a reassignment: Soon __ 1–2 years __ Future __
Not sure __
Explain:

C. My short-term (1–3 years) career development plans and goals are:

D. My long-term (over 3 years) career development plans and goals are:

E. Other things I'd like to discuss at mid-year:

PART V

Project Management

Project management's responsibilities are the same as general management's responsibilities: planning, staffing, organizing, leading, and monitoring. Project control primarily includes the planning and monitoring responsibilities. In Chapter 11, a basic project control procedure is explained. The ten steps apply to both MIS and non-MIS projects. Although there is a consensus on the approach, many projects are not on schedule or budget because steps are missing or incomplete.

The procedure obviously applies to projects with predefined phases; however, since level 4 prototypes (see Chapter 14) are now more prevalent, what control procedures are best suited for this less structured environment? Consider the publication of a standard life cycle Design Document versus a prototype working model of an on-line system. In both cases, the milestone is final approval of the design. The tasks required for the milestone were different, but task definitions and estimates were possible for both approaches. This logic applies to each of the ten steps although expectations are less for prototypes. The point is that management should consciously select the project control tools for prototype projects such as Work Plans, Gantt Charts, Pert Charts, and Budgets.

Seven of the nine productivity measures defined in Chapter 7 utilized LOC, Function Points, or man-days in the calculation. Chapter 12 provides further detail on the definitional options for each of these factors. The primary emphasis is on projects, although maintenance is also included. After the explanation of the importance of definitions, the Function Point measurement is explained, followed by an analysis of the four project characteristics influencing productivity in our environment.

In the industry, function points have replaced LOC as the preferred method of quantifying output. However, with end user computing and cooperative processing (client/server concept), there is far less interest in measuring output, rather, the focus is on business impact and the technology. Thus, only large organizations quantify output in their software factories with function points on LOC.

CHAPTER 11

Basic Project Control

The scope of this project control procedure is limited to the basic concepts. It deals with the fundamentals of control and is independent of project phase. The ten steps are divided in planning and monitoring segments. Figure 12.1 illustrates how the procedure relates to the basic working documents: Work Plan, PERT Chart, Gantt Chart, and Budget.

PLANNING A PROJECT

Step 1: Define Tasks. A written task description provides a common reference for all project members.

Having a one-line description of a task, the typical case, is adequate when the tasks are straightforward, such as, convert program to COBOL II; but a primary reason for project overruns is not elaborating on ambiguous tasks. For example, consider the task "Enhance database and reports." This description is too general and might be interpreted as a change to one or two fields or a complete redesign of the database.

Missing tasks and poorly documented tasks are major contributions to late and overbudget projects. Standard life cycle methodologies provide a checklist of tasks for each project phase.

FIGURE 11.1. Project Control Schematic.

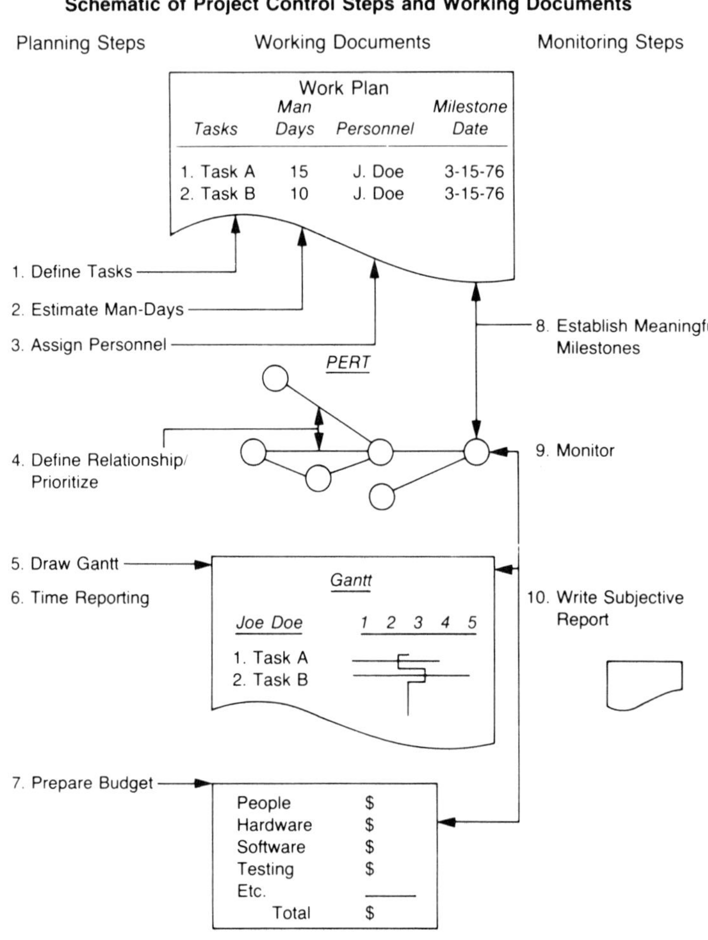

Because system requirements are not firm, the probability of overlooking tasks is highest in the first two phases (feasibility and design).

Written task descriptions provide greater value when different organizational groups become involved. In some situations, greater documentation is required, in others, more documentation is a paper drill. Management judgement must dictate the appropriate balance.

Step 2: Estimate Man-Days. Estimating the time to accomplish a task is the second step. A standard definition of time provides necessary consistency. *Man-days* is a generic title for the following: hours, days, weeks, months, or years.

When knowledge is incomplete, the typical situation early in a project, Project Managers resist this step, especially written estimates. Although not intuitive, the sum of the detail task man-days is less than the project or macro estimate. The primary reason is unknown or missing tasks, which, by definition, include no man-day estimates. Many Project Managers factor an allowance for unknowns when summing task man-days to total project man-days.

Step 3: Assign Personnel. When assigning personnel to tasks, consideration should be given to experience and talents of individuals. Man-day estimates in step 2 were made assuming an average experience level. If inexperienced individuals are on the project, man-day estimates should be adjusted. Time should be allowed for training new personnel on technical skills. Also, a one-month project orientation period is generally required.

After tasks are assigned, total the man-days for each person. Compare this total to the available days. If an imbalance exists among individuals, tasks should be reassigned. This comparison may appear obvious, but it is frequently overlooked.

Step 4: Define Task Relationships and Priority. Since resources are finite, all tasks cannot be accomplished concurrently. Priority tasks are either on the critical path or involve problem areas.

When unique task relationships are minimal, say 15 or less, it is sufficient to note the precedence on the work plan. If more unique relationships exist, a PERT chart is recommended. When charting large projects, the scope of one PERT chart should be 50 activities or less, since too much detail causes confusion. If a project has 300 activities, modular PERTs, representing a segment of the project, maintain simplicity. The greatest value of a PERT chart is the planning and thinking required to prepare it, assuring the planners understand the relationships. In most cases, modifications do not require redrawing the chart. A project manager's main concern when deviations occur is correcting the problem.

There exist a number of software packages for automating the PERT process as well as documenting steps (1-6). In the proper situation, automation can save time, but as discussed in step 6, packages require time to learn conventions and input data.

Step 5: Draw Gantt Charts. Gantt tasks in priority order, considering relationships among tasks. Since individuals usually work on multiple tasks and may have other responsibilities, elapsed days are greater than task man-day estimates. To assure that available man-days equal Gantted man-days, total the man-days Gantted for the period and compare the result with the available man-days. For example:

Gantt Individual A	Gantted Man-Days	Ten Available Days: Week One (1 2 3 4 5)	Week Two (6 7 8 9 10)
Task 1	3	days 1–5 ——→	
Task 2	3	days 4–5 ——	——→ day 9
Task 3	4	days 1–5 ——	——→ day 10
	10		

Note that elapsed time exceeds man-days in each case, but 10 man-days of tasks require 10 elapsed days.

Step 6: Time-Reporting. Do employees account for their time by recording hours to pre-defined tasks? In MIS organizations, time-reporting via an automated system is the rule rather than the exception. Project management is one reason for time-reporting, although other valid reasons exist, such as charge back or recording department statistics. Many software packages that automate time-reporting are also capable of generating Gantt and PERT charts or have the sophistication to simulate project alternatives. These additional capabilities are not free. They require additional inputs, such as individual skills and task completions, relationships, priorities, and cost. Because of these requirements, probably less than 5 percent of all projects benefit from a completely automated approach. Organizational environment and management philosophy dictate the degree of automation.

Step 7: Prepare Budget. Project budgets include dollars for people, hardware, software, testing, conversion, etc. In our environment, staff expense usually dominates the total. The burdened rate for an individual is about $300 per day. During the implementation phase, $100 per day is added for hardware-testing resources. If new hardware or expensive software is purchased, it would become a significant budget item. Our standard procedure is not to monitor expenses other than man-days during the life cycle. Thus, project control budgets are not prepared although all costs are included in the feasibility/general design proposal.

Step 8: Establish Meaningful Milestones. A meaningful milestone is a point in time when a task or number of tasks can be completed 100 percent. The following are examples:

1. Report package documentation sign-off
2. Completion of the system test plan
3. Phase I implementation

One important factor, which is often overlooked when milestones are defined, is an explanation of how and who will sign off on the milestone. When milestones are defined, specify how the tasks will be acknowledged complete and who will sign off on the completion.

Step 9: Monitor. There are two types of monitoring: individual and project. Individual monitoring is best done by updating Gantt charts with a line showing current status versus expected status at a point in time. Monitoring actual man-hours expended versus planned is also possible, as shown in Fig. 11.2.

Project monitoring is based on the pre-defined milestones. It is very important to reconcile variations from each milestone. If the first milestone date is missed by a considerable margin, then there may be good reason to reevaluate all the remaining projections. This step implies that the Project Manager: understands the tasks, knows why deviations from the plan occur, and takes appropriate action to correct out-of-control situations.

Extensive project control procedures can have an adverse impact on productivity. Good project control is not elaborate control. When dates slip, there is a tendency to over-control and define detailed procedures. For example, instead of monitoring overall progress weekly or monthly, a procedure to monitor progress day by day may be implemented. Thus, individuals and the Project Manager would have to maintain considerable detail data in an attempt to report on a daily basis. Even more important than the extra time required for elaborate controls is the fact that they can divert the attention of a Project Manager from the relevant issue of finding the real problem.

Success is not dependent on detail reporting. Procedures should not be a burden on Project Managers, but rather an extension of their control techniques. Assuming the basic steps are followed, there are as many variations as there are Project Managers. Some individuals find it difficult to write concise reports, and others work effectively with rough Gantt charts and note cards. The point is, a control procedure should not force Project Managers to standardize all aspects of their jobs. Productivity is greatest when a Project Manager sticks with the fundamentals and is allowed to function in a personally effective manner.

Step 10: Write Subjective Reports. In addition to the objective measures above, a subjective report should be completed periodically by the individual responsible for the project. Numbers and charts do not describe the attitude or motivation of the project team. It has been said that individuals on a successive project always have a "warm feeling" about the progress. A subjective report represents a personal appraisal of the project status.

SKIPPING STEPS

Although there is consensus on the value of the ten step project control procedure, only a few of the steps are used routinely. Is this wrong? Not necessarily. Consider the example below which was extracted from a computer installation plan:

Functional Area	*Item Description*	*Resp. Group*	*Target Date*	*Status, Notes & Dependencies*
Change Control	Create change control entries	CPM	08/18/89	Completed
	Schedule Operations Availability with all user areas (manufacturing)	OPNS	08/22/89	
Preparation of Facilities	Provide information on console configurations	Vendor	08/18/89	Completed
	Schedule and move the 3174 cntlrs.	SM OPNS	08/20/89	Completed
	Schedule electrical support	SM	08/18/89	Completed

Six steps are missing: estimate man days, define relationships (high level ones implied, i.e. preparatory activities precede implementation and audit activities), gantt chart, time reporting, budget, and subjective report. However, the four remaining steps are adequate for the situation. This example illustrates how judgement applies to project control; four steps sufficed—task definition, assign personnel, set milestones, and monitor.

SUMMARY

The ten steps, seven for Planning and three for Monitoring, apply to any phase of a project. As those who have managed projects know, project control is not easy; it requires hard work, good judgement, and a basic procedure. Proper execution of the ten fundamental steps is the answer.

REFERENCES

Johnson, James R. *Advanced Project Control*, Journal of Systems Management, May 1977, pp. 24–27.

Johnson, James R. *Managing for Productivity in Data Processing*, 1980, pp. 43–49.

CHAPTER 12

Lines of Code/Function Points

As experienced managers acknowledge, productivity is a function of selecting qualified people, establishing an adequate working environment, motivating personnel, and providing the proper management direction. When a group of individuals achieves high productivity, a positive atmosphere exists. Even though productivity may not be measured, those associated with the project know productivity is high. Optimal productivity is a result of dedicated, involved individuals working on "their" system. The adage "Put your heart in your work" still applies in the computer age. Management's responsibility is to provide individuals with this opportunity. Thus, it is concluded that managing is only a motivating process, not a productivity-measuring activity, right?

Not completely. Faith is no longer an attribute of higher management; as maintenance and overhead increase, justification of budget increases becomes more difficult, and higher level management is making the message clear: Show us your productivity increases.

Part III (Chapter 7) explained how the factory monitors performance with five productivity measures, two quality measures, and two estimating measures. Seven of the calculations use either Lines of Code (LOC), man-days, or Function Points. This chapter provides additional background on each, including our rules. The final Function Point analysis isolated four project characteristics key to productivity. Before clarifying LOC, a review of the factory product is appropriate.

THE FACTORY PRODUCT

There are programs and there are programs. Depending on the definition of *program*, the cost of one may be nine times the cost of another. As Fred Brooks explains in *Mythical Man-Month* (1975), programs exist at four levels of complexity:

Level	*Type of Program*	*Cost Factor*
1	program	1X
2	programming product	3X
3	programming system	3X
4	programming system product	9X

According to this definition, a *program* is run only by its author for a specific purpose. A *programming product* is differentiated from a program in two ways: It is generalized and it is documented. Going from level one to level two increases the cost by a factor of three.

A *programming system* is a component that must be integrated, along with other components, into a system. Having to resolve interfaces increases the development cost over the cost to develop a program by an additional factor of three.

In the Software Factory environment, the fourth level of complexity is the product. It has the attributes of both a programming system and a programming product. A *programming system product* requires nine times more resources than a program of similar size. The system is generalized, documented, integrated, and independent of its writers.

Implied in the term *cost* is a programming rate of production based on LOC. In other words, if nine LOC per hour were generated writing programs (the first level), then a productivity rate for a programming system product of one LOC per hour would be expected.

A LINE OF CODE

Definitions can account for vast differences in LOC reported by different organizations. For example, if only verbs (procedural statements) are counted as LOC, the totals are approximately one-third of all LOC. Establishing LOC rules for counting is an arbitrary task, and rules vary by organization; however, consistency is the key factor allowing comparison among different groups and comparisons over time. For our statistics, an LOC is: A source statement corresponding to a line on a coding sheet. More specifically, the options and our choices:

Procedural Statements	Yes
Copylib (data definitions)	Yes (once per system)
Program Comments	Yes
External Documentation	No
Job Control Language	Yes
Conversion Programs	No

Applying these counting rules to new programs is straightforward. But, unfortunately, most projects involve changing or deleting existing code, programs, or entire systems. Thus additional rules are required for enhancements, those projects impacting existing systems. For changes made within a program, experience showed that two times more effort was required than writing new LOC. Thus, added LOC in production programs were multiplied by two. The same logic was used for replacing LOC, with each one counting as two. The last option within a program is to delete an LOC. Obviously, program analysis and testing is required so the rule was count each deleted LOC as one. These rules were programmed into an automated system which quarterly ran against production libraries and totaled procedural statements and program comments. To account for copylibs (data definitions) and Job Control Language (JCL), the LOC counts are increased by 15 percent based on averages statistics (10 percent copylib and 5 percent JCL).

If an entire production program is deleted, should it be counted as productive work? The options are: Yes, No, or Count a percentage. Our rule was to count 50 percent because considerable effort is required to validate the remaining parts of a system when one piece has been deleted.

The above rules apply to "LOC activity" as used in productivity measure four. Different rules applied to "protect LOC implemented" for productivity measure two, reference Chapter 9, Results section.

COUNTING MAN-DAYS

It is not obvious, but counting man days can be as confusing as counting LOC. Consider the options: project phases, managers, end-user effort, administrative time, technical support, training, etc. Our definition is as follows:

All project phases	Yes
Direct project personnel	Yes
Administrative time	No
Project Manager time	No
Secretarial time	No
Technical Support time	No
End-User time	No
Project training	Yes
General training	No

Thus, when project man-days total 125, the total includes direct time reported by project personnel for all phases of the project, feasibility study through implementation.

WHAT IS A FUNCTION POINT?

The Function Points technique measures an application by counting its external inquiries, inputs, and outputs, as well as master files and interfaces to other applications. The methodology assigns numeric values to user deliverables. Since it measures external functions produced, the technique is independent of the programming language or other technology. To illustrate, consider Projects A and B:

	A (COBOL)	B (4GL)
Man-Days	100	20
LOC	8000	1600
Function Points	125	125

The productivity as defined by LOC/man-day is identical (8000/100 = 1600/20); however, Project A required five times the man-days. The Function Point metric documents five times greater productivity: for Project B, 6.25 Function Points/man-day versus 1.25 Function Points/man-day for Project A. Thus, language dependency, the primary disadvantage of LOC, is not a problem. The components of the Function Point calculation are:

(1)		(2)		(3)		(4)		(5)
Project Elements	×	Weight Factors	=	Total Function Points	×	Degree of Complexity	=	Total Adjusted Function Points

Project Elements, the first factor above, are composed of five entities:

Inputs, which provide user communication to an application: input documents, terminal screens, keyed input, scanner data.
Outputs, which provide user communication from an application: printed reports, terminal printed output, operator messages.
Inquiry, which is a direct search for specific information using a key or retrieval logic.
Master Files, which comprise each logical file grouping of data from the viewpoint of the user.
Interface, which includes major automated interfaces to other applications that are not transactions.

As shown in Figure 12.1, the number of each entity is recorded and multiplied by Weight Factors to obtain the total Function Points per element. The weights are the same for inputs and inquiries but increase progressively for outputs, interfaces and master files. (For simplicity, the description and example excludes levels of difficulty for each entity.)

FIGURE 12.1. Technique for obtaining total Function Points per project element.

Project Elements	*Number*	*Weight*		*FP*
Inputs	2	4	=	8
Outputs	5	5	=	25
Inquiry	5	4	=	20
Master Files	4	10	=	40
Interface	3	7	=	21
				114

Complexity Factors:

Communication Facilities	5
Online Processing	5
Complex Processing Logic	2
Multiple Sites	5
Conversion Difficulty	5
New Hardware	3
Remote Users	5
	30*

Total Function Points	×	*Degree of Complexity*	=	*Total Adjusted Function Points*
114	×	[.8 + (30 × .01)*]	=	
114	×	1.1	=	125

*20 considered average [.8 + (20 × .01)] = 1.0

The degree of complexity is considered separately because it measures system implementation difficulty. From a user's viewpoint, technical complexity may be transparent; but from a DP standpoint, an innovative high-technology project will require additional resources. The primary complexity factors are: communications facilities, distributed processing, high volumes, performance objectives, on-line processing, complex processing logic, multiple sites, conversion difficulty, new hardware, new software/database, and remote users.

Each of these factors is given a value from zero to five depending on the level of influence (0—no influence, 5—strong influence). An example clarifies the procedure: Project A and B above both produced 125 Function Points as calculated in Figure 12.1.

In actual practice, one to four hours are required to compute a Function Points index for a one man-year project. The index is prepared shortly after completion of the implementation phase. Consistency is best served when all Function Points index assignments are reviewed by one individual.

Unforeseen questions continue to arise, perhaps how to treat a novel multipurpose screen design or a multiformat report. These issues are resolved and documented for reference to ensure proper point assignments in the future. Periodically, the accumulated Function Points data can be analyzed to reveal productivity trends over time.

COMPARISON OF LOC AND FUNCTION POINTS

Which measure is better, LOC or Function Points? If projects are developed in different languages, the Function Point method is the preferred alternative; but if the programming language is the same, then both measures are valuable, correlating well on the majority of projects. Once counting rules are defined for an automated counting system, the LOC reports are objective, consistent statistics. The Function Points methodology has inherent subjectivity in the assignment of weights and complexity factors. Also, the calculation favors systems with many input/output interfaces versus systems with extensive processing logic. With either LOC or Function Points, it should be remembered that system quality or corporate contribution are not included.

ANALYSIS WITH FUNCTION POINTS

Since 1983, projects have been analyzed in an attempt to explain why they produce different LOC rates and Function Point output. If a correlation exists between one or more project characteristic and output (either LOC or Function Points), then these characteristics could be used when estimating future projects.

In pursuing the data from over 100 projects, the variability was surprising, especially considering the stability of one organization. In a typical year, Function Points per man-day varied from .16 to 2.43 (15 times) and LOC per man-day varied from 6 to 266 (44 times).

In our first analysis of Function Point and LOC data, one or more characteristics did not correlate well. The characteristics considered: personnel expertise (both MIS and user), project size, percent new code, and system complexity. This lack of correlation contradicts intuition. Characteristics should predict productivity as measured by Function Points and LOC; after all, commercial estimating packages use project characteristics as a base.

What we discovered when revisiting the issue was that the characteristics do determine productivity, but not the same characteristics for each project. In other words, a project generally has one or two overriding factors, "dominant" characteristics, influencing productivity. For example, if a complete system or large percent of the programs are cloned, productivity may be high even though complex processing, a characteristic that lowers productivity, is also present. Thus, the weight of a characteristic varies by project, and numerical averages do not correlate with productivity.

The four characteristics controlling productivity were:

	Productivity	
	Higher	*Lower*
1. Screens	Many	Few
2. Cloning	Extensive	Limited
3. Processing	Simple	Complex
4. Integration	Limited	Extensive

After the projects were sequenced by Function Point productivity, they were divided into three ranges: Low (.12 to .53 Function Points/man-day), Medium (.63 to .89 Function Points/ man-day), and High (1.0 to 3.89 Function Points/man-day). (See Figure 12.2.)

FIGURE 12.2. Function Points per man-day sequence.

	MDAYS	*FP*	*FP/MD*	*Screens*	*Cloning*	*Processing*	*Integration*
LOW							
One	505	60	.12			Complex	Extensive
Two	239	60	.25	Few		Complex	
Three	174	45	.26	Few		Complex	
Four	168	48	.29	Few		Complex	
Five	1982	677	.34	Few		Complex	
Six	89	31	.35	Few		Complex	
Seven	114	43	.38				Extensive
Eight	231	91	.39			Complex	Extensive
Nine	1327	568	.43			Complex	
Ten	359	160	.45	Few	Limited		
Eleven	351	162	.46	Few	Limited		
Twelve	168	81	.48	Few			
Thirteen	244	122	.50			Complex	
Fourteen	85	45	.53	Few			
MEDIUM							
One	461	291	.63				
Two	592	372	.63				
Three	239	162	.68	}			
Four	380	258	.68	}			
Five	4393	3005	.68	}			
				}	No dominant characteristic		
Six	148	105	.71	}			
Seven	115	83	.72	}			
Eight	109	84	.77	}			
Nine	414	338	.82				
Ten	101	86	.85				
Eleven	1118	998	.89				
HIGH							
One	282	281	1.00		Extensive		
Two	181	194	1.07				Limited
Three	1052	1179	1.12	Many			Limited
Four	119	270	2.27	Many	Extensive		
Five	448	1743	3.89		*		

*Purchased software

By using the four characteristics along with the dominant theory, virtually all productivity differences could be explained. The same analysis was performed for LOC productivity with equally successful results.

REFERENCES

Brooks, Fred. *Mythical Man-Month.* Addison-Wesley, Reading, Mass., 1975.

PART VI

The Weakest Link

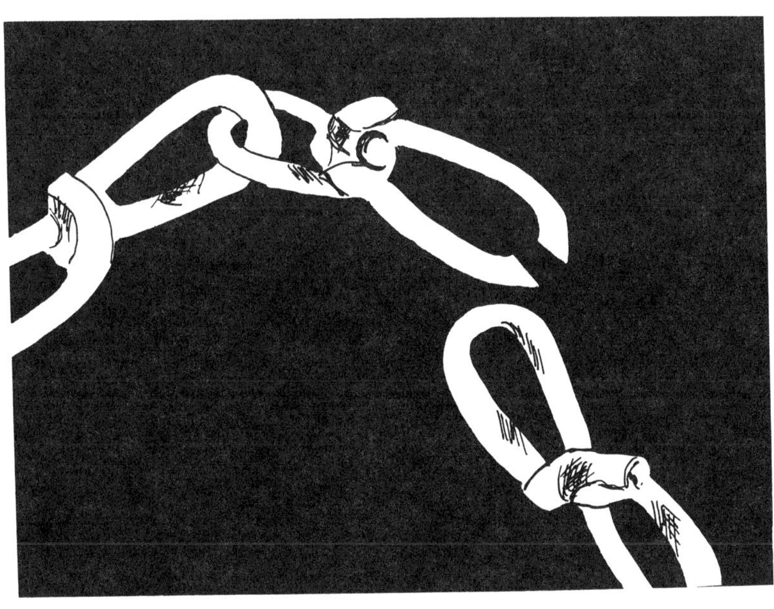

Consistent subsecond response time and computer availability are critical to productivity. Our concentrated research into the subject started years ago, when subsecond response time was first realized. After comprehending the productivity gains, I was amazed. Why didn't the industry believe the results? Publicity was minimal.

In reviewing the conclusions with Walter Doherty and Bucky Pope from IBM's Thomas Watson Research Center, I learned they had similar thoughts. Thus, the goal of Chapter 13 is to "prove" the value of response time. A simple technique for any organization to validate the impact of subsecond response time is provided. Appendix C, the Thadhani curve, supplements Chapter 13. It is recommended to those interested in more supporting detail on measuring sub-second response time.

Recording computer availability as viewed from the end user's terminal is a difficult task. Commonly quoted availability statistics seldom reflect the actual time a user can execute all transactions. A complete chain, composed of both hardware and software links (components), must exist for end-user availability. As hardware reliability improves, the weakest links become the software components. Topics included: calculating availability with independent components, external monitoring of availability, and alternative hardware/software options.

CHAPTER 13

Response Time and Availability

Having studied computer System Response Time (SRT) and availability for a number of years, we have concluded that both directly link to productivity. Surprising productivity gains, gains dwarfing other productivity programs, are possible. This conclusion is based on detail analysis in our software factory environment but applies to all knowledge workers using the computer for a significant part of their jobs; we have over two thousand knowledge workers using office automation and business applications.

In our Software Factory of over two hundred knowledge workers, when average SRT dropped from 1.7 seconds in 1983 to .76 seconds in 1986, productivity as measured in transactions per hour increased 42 percent, a productivity value of over $4 million in base payroll. Many organizations have an opportunity for productivity improvements equal to or greater than our results by lowering SRT and/or increasing computer availability.

Availability, as viewed by knowledge workers at a terminal, is difficult to measure because host statistics record individual component failure, not the resulting impact on terminal users. External monitoring by a PC is one way to obtain availability statistics. Various components form connecting links in two chains; a break in one link of either chain, and the knowledge worker cannot function. Modern technology has produced a stronger hardware chain, but complexity in the software environment isn't making the goal of high availability much easier. If service level agreements supporting high availability are not maintained with host computers, other alternatives should be explored.

SYSTEM RESPONSE TIME

As an introduction to SRT, consider the following statements:

- Subsecond response time directly improves productivity.
- In most organizations, proving the link between subsecond response time and increased productivity is possible.

Before explaining why each of these statements is true, a definition of SRT is appropriate. Consider a person at a computer terminal (or personal computer) entering inquiry or update transactions to a host computer, as with an airline reservation system. The time from when the person depresses Enter until a response is displayed is SRT. It includes time for the computer to process the request and communicate back to the terminal. The average SRT of .76 seconds quoted above is an average for all transactions entered on the terminal. Productivity is measured by the number of transactions entered per sign-on hour per person. At .76 second SRT, the productivity rate was 331 transactions per hour for each of the 100 knowledge workers concurrently on the computer.

Do You Believe?

"I've observed individuals on terminals, and, in a quarter of a second, a person can't read the screen and decide on what to do next. Thus, subsecond SRT is a myth."

This reaction demonstrates a basic misunderstanding of the relationship between SRT and transactions per hour. Let's work backwards, starting with 331 transactions per hour, and compute the average time between transactions.

$$3600\,\frac{\text{sec}}{\text{hr}} \div 331\,\frac{\text{trans}}{\text{hr}} = 10.9\,\frac{\text{seconds}}{\text{transaction}}$$

The majority of the 10.9 seconds is user think/input time. For our data, 10.14 seconds think/input and only .76 seconds SRT (see Figure 13.1 for schematic). In a programming environment, a realistic goal for a large staff is 400 transactions per hour equating to 9 seconds between transactions. Actually, the work pattern is not as uniform as implied. Rather, individuals work in spurts. They develop a sequence of actions in memory and then wait on system response to execute the actions. This is why consistent subsecond response time is so important; if the thought process is disrupted, the sequence of actions must be developed again in an individual's memory.

Two key concepts are *user rhythm* and *consistency*. Data shows that lower SRT averages are accompanied by more consistent response time (smaller standard deviation). Thus, individuals are able to develop a rhythm of quick action based on anticipated consistent subsecond response. Inconsistent response is equivalent to personal distractions or interruptions. When below one second,

FIGURE 13.1. Schematic of relationship between SRT and transactions per hour.

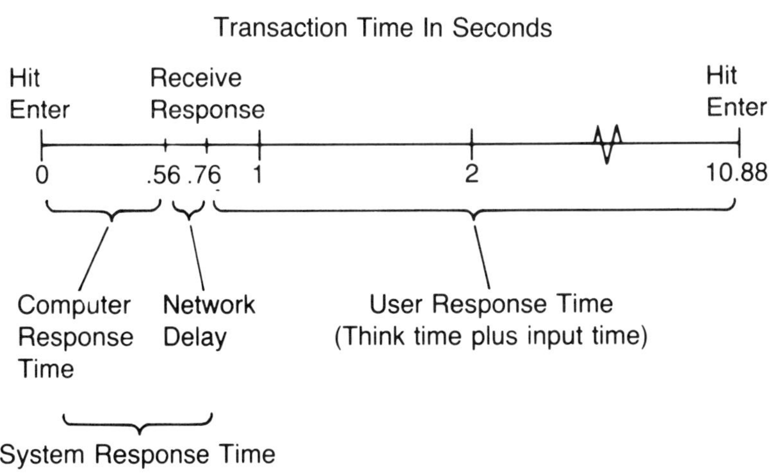

If the average transaction elapsed time is 10.88 seconds, 331 transactions per hour are processed: $\frac{3600 \text{ sec.}}{\text{hr.}} \div \frac{331 \text{ trans.}}{\text{hr.}} = \frac{10.88 \text{ sec.}}{\text{trans.}}$

the smaller standard deviation is a very important aspect of subsecond SRT.

On an office automation and business application (accounts payable, order input, billing, etc.), the amount of productivity gain is related to transaction complexity, volume, and the reliance on the computer to complete work. Thus, the value of subsecond SRT depends on the environment and, in certain situations, will exceed the productivity computed for the programming/design environment.

Other arguments used to discredit subsecond SRT are:

1. IBM, a firm profiting from hardware sales, has published the studies.
2. The curve just shows that people change their work habits as response time is reduced, relying more on the computer.
3. Experience and training have more impact on transactions per hour than SRT.
4. The transactions per hour rate does not directly relate to group productivity.

The first statement is obviously true; however, it is not a reason to disregard the analysis. IBM has devoted considerable time to studying response time. Its staff at the Thomas Watson Research Center is acknowledged as world experts on the subject. In compiling our data, we validated their methodology and results, substantiating that sub-second SRT dramatically improves productivity.

That individuals may change work habits as SRT changes is also true, but this is not a significant distortion of the measurement in our environment. This was proven by monitoring the types of transactions as defined by computer resources consumed (human-intensive versus computer-intensive). The maximum variance for human-intensive transactions was 2.7 percent (91.3 to 88.6) over five years. If individuals change work habits to become more productive, then subsecond SRT produces an additional benefit.

Experience is, no doubt, a key to productivity. Although our detailed data shows significant variation among individuals of similar experience, some people are simply more productive than others. This is an independent fact. Subsecond SRT improves productivity at all experience levels.

Do individual transactions per hour relate to group productivity? For Software Factory work, this is a difficult question to answer conclusively because MIS projects are nonrepetitive; however, our primary productivity measure, Lines of Code (LOC), correlates very well with transactions per hour rates over the four-year period, as in Figure 13.2: a 55 percent decrease in SRT (1.7 – .76 seconds) produced increases in transactions per hour (42 percent), LOC per project man-year (32 percent), and LOC per support person (32 percent).

FIGURE 13.2 Correlation of LOC measurement with transactions per hour.

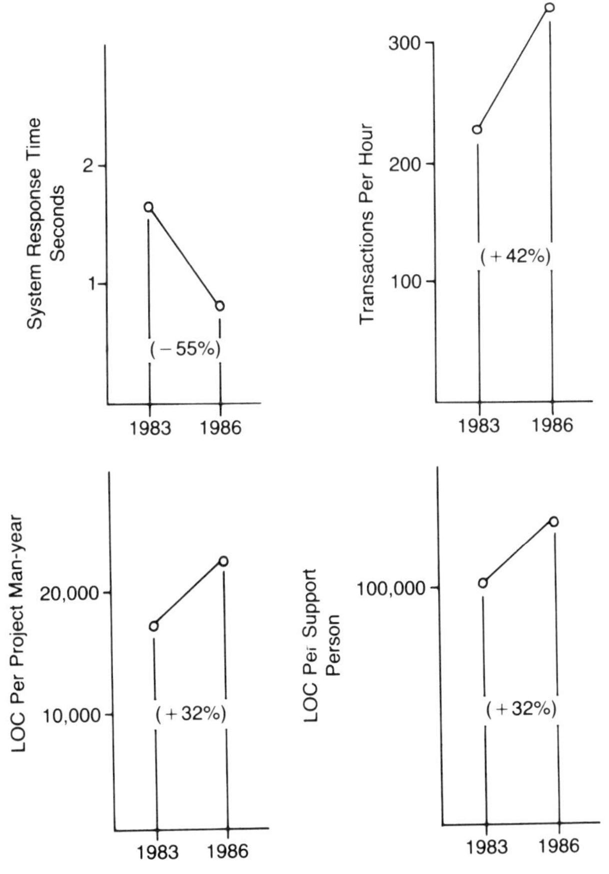

Assuming an exact relationship, an unrealistic assumption, an SRT improvement of 55 percent for one-half of the working time would increase productivity 27.5 percent (55 percent ÷ 2) versus the recorded 42 percent and 32 percent. Since additional functions were performed on the terminal and since other productivity tools were implemented during the same period, the two productivity measures would not be expected to match exactly. Also, over this period, the sign-on hours per person increased from three hours to four hours.

Our data substantiates a previous IBM study of identical projects with different SRT documented in the *IBM Systems Journal* (Vol. 23, No. 1, 1984). As SRT decreased 62 percent (2.22 – .84 seconds), transactions per hour increased 61 percent (160 – 258), and LOC per project man-year 65 percent (14,720 – 24,300). Granted, there are definitional discrepancies between our data and IBM's, but the results directly link transactions per hour and lines of code productivity.

Your Own Validation

Not every organization has historical information as presented for consecutive years. However, the relationship between SRT and transactions per hour can be validated by comparing performance statistics for prime time (8 A.M. - 5 P.M.) and non-prime time (off-peak hours). In non-prime time, the system has fewer users, so the computer resource provides lower SRT. Consider the recent data from our organization (August, 1987):

	Prime Time	*Non-Prime Time*	*Percent*
SRT (seconds)	.82	.62	(24%)
Transactions per Hour	266	338	27%

The data should be available in most organizations from resource management facilities (RMF for IBM mainframes). For all knowledge workers signed on, the following is summarized: number of sign-on hours, number of transactions, average SRT for the transactions. The transactions per hour recorded in 1987 are lower than the 1986 data because, starting in October, 1986, terminals could access two systems at the same time. However, when comparing prime time and non-prime time during one month, the environment is identical.

Remote Terminals

Unless a special high-speed line is used, knowledge workers on remote terminals have a problem, since subsecond response time is not possible.

If terminals are connected to local controllers, the typical response time delay for a screen is between .1 and .2 seconds. At typical remote transmission speeds (2,400 baud modems), five to six seconds are required for a full screen. When only one or two lines are transmitted, the typical delay is .5 seconds, possibly doubling SRT (computer and network delay). Remote response delays reduce productivity by 50 to 100 transactions per hour per person, an astounding loss to the corporation.

A high-capacity line can reduce the transmission by 100 times, down to .1 second, the low range for local controllers. Thus, two action items are: for local controllers, monitor the activity to assure no bottlenecks, and for remote computing, use the highest capacity line possible.

Quantifying Response Time

Since SRT determines transactions per hour and since transactions per hour reflect productivity, the value of improved SRT for a group of knowledge workers is calculated by multiplying the percent increase in transactions times the knowledge workers' salary:

$$\begin{matrix}\text{Transaction} \\ \text{Rate Increase} \\ \text{(Percent)}\end{matrix} \times \begin{matrix}\text{Salary of} \\ \text{Knowledge Workers} \\ \text{Using Computer}\end{matrix} = \begin{matrix}\text{Value of Improved} \\ \text{Response Time}\end{matrix}$$

For our prime/non-prime data:

$$\frac{338\text{-}266}{266} \times (\$50{,}000 \times 100) = \$1{,}350{,}000$$

In headcount reduction, for a staff of 200 with 50 percent of their activity on the terminal, this equates to over 25 people.

Does staff actually decrease in most organizations as response time improves? No. In the typical situation, more work is produced by the same number of people.

Cost of Hardware

Which is more valuable—human time at the terminal or the computer resources consumed? IBM says that human resources are 10 to 35 times more expensive than computer resources. For the conservative estimate, human expense is an order of magnitude greater than computer expense for the time an individual is at the terminal. Our data shows a similar result. Of the total billable cost for systems development services, 80 percent is payroll both direct and indirect. Sixteen percent is hardware, with 2 percent for non-payroll and 2 percent for facilities. The 12.5:1 ratio supports the concept of high availability and subsecond response based on terminal hours that average four hours per person. The ratio indicates how hardware dollars leverage payroll dollars.

AVAILABILITY

Is it easier to provide subsecond SRT for human intensive transactions or to provide 98 percent availability? The answer is dependent on the amount of hardware and, more importantly, software components required for availability and their reliability. In the majority of sophisticated operating environments, the 98 percent availability is far more difficult to provide.

On-line availability is the time a user can sign on and perform a desired function on a terminal divided by the work day time. For example, if the user's view of the system is down for 10 minutes on an eight-hour day, then availability is 98 percent (470/480 min.).

Aspects of Availability

There are two surprising and misunderstood aspects of availability. First, when all components are needed, user availability is a multiplication of each component's availability; and second, host monitoring systems do not provide complete availability statistics. Consider the components in the chain of availability for a programmer developing an on-line database system:

Operating system
Region controlling terminals
Test on-line network
Time-sharing option (TSO)
Database
Hardware
General software
Number of sign-ons

If each of these eight components independently has an availability of 99%, the combined user availability is 99 percent eight times itself, or 91.4 percent. This is a staggering 42 minutes of unavailability in an eight-hour day. To achieve an end-user availability of 98 percent, each of the components must have individual availability of 99.8 percent. With the new software releases and fixes required by the modern large-scale systems, availability is impacted primarily by software. Ask operations managers with responsibility for managing both large-scale (IBM 3090) and small-scale (IBM AS400, 4300) systems which size is more reliable. The smaller systems have far better records, not because individual hardware components are better, but because the software complexity is less on the smaller systems.

The second surprising aspect of availability is measurement complexities. Because of the multiple hardware and software components required for user functions, host statistics on availability are inadequate. They report availability by independent component rather than from the knowledge worker's view, a view requiring a combination of components. In other words, the multiplicity impact is ignored. Partial components of failure occur and are also not reported. For example, assume an on-line customer address database is inaccessible due to a late batch pass. All availability reports show the software operating, yet Accounts Payable personnel attempting to use terminal transactions requiring the database will not execute, a major disruption to their operation. The late pass may or may not have been documented depending on the cause: application program bug, hardware, operating system, capacity, etc.

The second measurement complexity concerns the recovery time after software or hardware failures. If the operating system is unavailable for 20 minutes, 20 minutes may be the reported downtime. However, the network software, the database software, or the database files may each add 5 minutes or more to the 20 minutes, producing a total of 35 minutes, the actual nonavailability from the user's view.

For the priority applications, it is possible to program a PC linked to a mainframe periodically executing typical transactions during working hours reporting transaction availability. This type of terminal monitor, a relatively new approach, is not constrained by the complexities encountered by host monitoring tools.

Value

To quantify the value of availability, consider user activity when the system is unavailable for five minutes. The knowledge worker's train of thought is lost along with the transaction in progress. Thus, when the system becomes available, the user must repeat the thought process lost during the 5 minutes. This may require 10 seconds or 5 minutes. Also, since the duration of downtime cannot be anticipated, another 10 seconds to 5 minutes of time may be lost because the user doesn't know when the system is available. Thus, the 5 minutes of unavailability becomes, at best case, 5 minutes 20 seconds and, at worst case, 15 minutes—three times the reported unavailability! As the unavailable time extends to, say, 30 minutes, a more typical figure for a major system, the extra lost time becomes a smaller percentage. For example, 30 minutes plus 10 minutes is only a 30 percent lost factor.

The general equation for calculating the lost work due to nonavailability is as follows:

$$\text{Average Salary Plus Benefits} \times \text{Average Percent Time Signed-On} \times \text{Number on Staff} \times \text{Extra Time Factor} \times \text{Nonavailability (100\%- Availability)} = \text{Lost Work}$$

The calculation is valid when the fraction of time signed-on is significant, and when the knowledge worker has difficulty shifting to tasks not requiring the computer. If shifts to noncomputer tasks are possible, the lost work is much less.

For our programming design environment with a staff of

200 signed-on 50 percent of the time, and assuming a conservative extra time factor (1.3, a 30 percent loss factor), an availability of .95 (.99 for five components) results in $325,000 lost work:

$$\$50{,}000 \times 50\% \times 200 \times 1.3 \times (100\% - 95\%) = \$325{,}000$$

Another way of stating this result: For each .01 improvement in availability, $65,000 is gained per year.

SERVICE-LEVEL OBJECTIVES

Our service-level objectives establish the expectations for host computer service for both SRT and availability:

- *SRT*—During prime time each day, less than one second average for all transactions, and less than .35 second average for human intensive transactions (about 90 percent of total).
- *Availability*—Ability of end user to perform desired function at least 98 percent of the time (nonavailable 10 minutes or less in an 8 hour period—prime time).

Terminal SRT service levels can be monitored with host software or terminal devices including PCs programmed to execute transactions. Figure 13.3 is a printout from IBM's NetView software for terminals during a one-week period processing over 1.5 million transactions. The average SRT is .78 seconds, with 89 percent processed in less than 1 second. Another technique is to program a PC to execute transactions periodically, say every 30 seconds, and record response time throughout the day.

As mentioned earlier, monitoring availability as seen by the user is a difficult task from the host. Using a PC executing selected transactions is a more reliable approach since it checks availability of files, networks, hardware, and software.

Meeting service-level objectives requires change control procedures, quality control, software tuning, and hardware capability. The more complex the environment, the more difficult the task. For subsecond SRT, the specific hardware recommendations are additional memory, solid-state paging, and disk-cache devices, along with high-capacity lines for remote communication (see Figure 13.4).

FIGURE 13.3 Printout from IBM's Net View software for terminals during a one-week period processing over 1.5 million transactions.

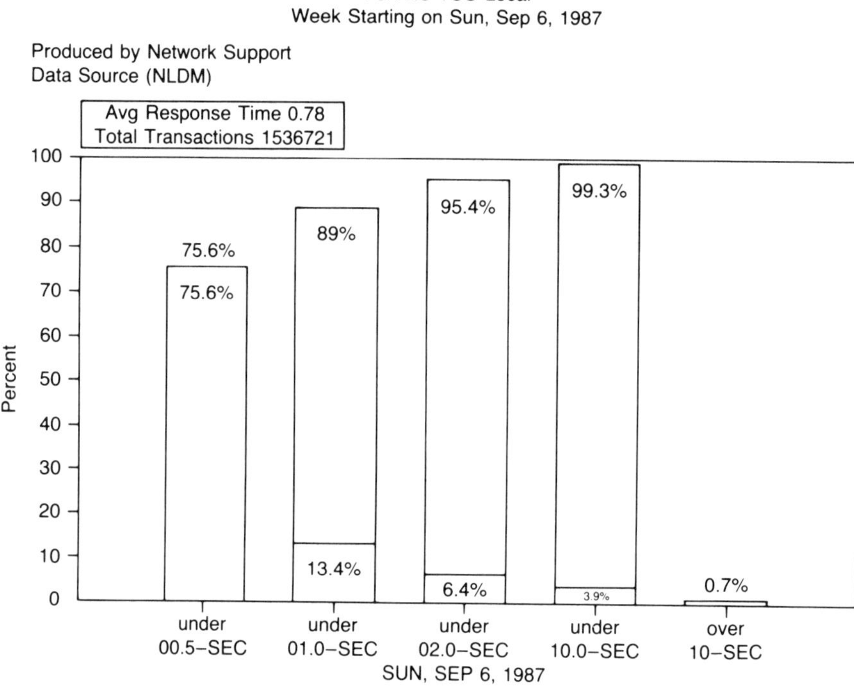

OTHER ALTERNATIVES

If there is agreement on the value of subsecond SRT for human intensive transactions and 98 percent availability, what alternatives exist if the host computer is not able to consistently provide the service?

Decentralization either with PCs for development personnel or departmental computers for business applications is one answer. The term *superior technology* has been applied to PC workstations; however, the label *simplified* technology is as appropriate because simplification is the reason for better response time. A PC user has a personal resource, and other users have no impact

FIGURE 13.4. Recommendations for subsecond SRT.

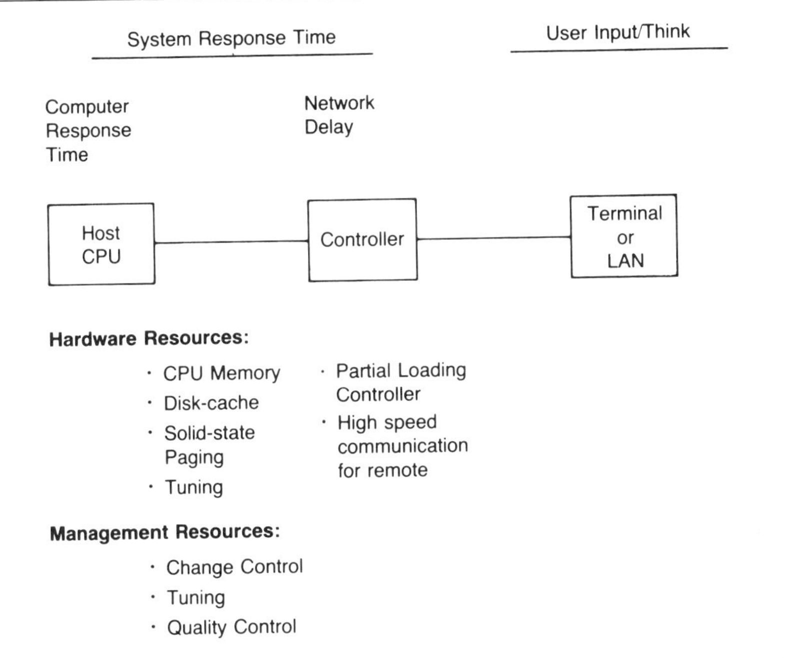

on response time or availability. Attach a local printer, and activities taking hours of elapsed time on a host only require minutes. Also, availability for PCs is documented at over 99.5 percent.

Sounds too good? What is the disadvantage? Data transfer between PC and host and software products for PCs are significant problems. In our environment, 23 percent of the work is independent word processing, a natural for improved productivity based on subsecond response time and high availability. Could PC workstations be justified for this portion of the work? Assume the following: host SRT for human intensive transactions .35 seconds, PC .25 seconds, host availability 95 percent, PC availability 99.5 percent. Then, for a staff of 200 that spends one-half its time on terminals, the value is $338,100 (see Figure 13.5).

Assuming equipment purchase of $4,000 per station and a $200,000 training cost (200 people × 5 days training at $50,000/year), an investment of $1 million ($800,000 + $200,000) pro-

FIGURE 13.5. Justifying a PC Workstation.

A. Editing Only

Response Time

$$50{,}000 \times \frac{400\text{-}345}{400} \times 100 \times 23\% \qquad = \$\ 158{,}125$$

Availability

$$50{,}000 \times 50\% \times 200 \times 1.3 \times .045 = \$292{,}500$$

$$\$292{,}500 \times 23\% \qquad = \$\ \ 67{,}275$$

Off-loading the Host
(4% of CPU to PC) = $ 112,700

$ 338,100

B. 75% Activities

Response Time

$$50{,}000 \times \frac{400\text{-}345}{400} \times 100 \times 75\% \qquad = \$\ 804{,}000$$

Availability

$$50{,}000 \times 50\% \times 200 \times 1.3 \times .045 = \$292{,}500$$

$$\$292{,}500 \times 75\% \qquad = \$\ 219{,}375$$

Off-loading the Host
(40% of CPU to PC) = $1,100,000

$2,123,373

duces a three-year payback. Not an especially good investment, although one worth considering.

However, if the majority of programming/design work, say 75 percent, could be done on the PC, the value increases dramatically to $2,223,373. A payback of less than six months! Can PC software support 75 percent of the activity for our complex environment? For our environment no, but, in a few years—probably yes. Note that the calculation is especially sensitive to the response time assumptions; in the computations, the host was delivering .35-second SRT, a value not consistently provided by many host facilities.

A similar analysis applies to departmental computers versus host service if the percent of non-host activities, such as word processing and independent applications, is substantial. Subsecond SRT and high availability may dictate a decentralized solution, especially since pass-through is possible to host data. The choice between centralization and decentralization must consider both response time and availability as product differences, if the two alternatives provide different service.

CONCLUSION

Subsecond SRT and improved availability for knowledge workers using terminals may provide double-digit productivity gains. Even though most executives don't appreciate the value of subsecond response time, all studies substantiate dramatic productivity gains as SRT decreases. Obtaining service levels of subsecond SRT for human intensive transactions and 98 percent availability involves management procedures and adequate hardware capacity. Monitoring service-level agreements provides a challenge especially for availability where using a PC to execute transactions is a new technique. The cost of people on terminals is over 10 times the cost of hardware resources consumed; thus, people productivity is leveraged by hardware.

In complex environments, it may not be possible to obtain service levels that assure productivity. If so, then other decentralized alternatives should be pursued. For our development activity, subsecond host SRT and high availability provide the best service option at this time. However, PC workstations may be logical alternatives to the host in two to three years.

REFERENCES

Doherty, W.J., and Pope, W.G. "Computing as a Tool for Human Augmentation." *IBM Systems Journal. 25*, 4 (1986). Reprint Order No. G321-5277.

Lambert, G.N. "A Comparative Study of Systems Response Time on Program Developer Productivity." *IBM Systems Journal, 23*, 1 (1984). Reprint Order No. G321-5208.

Lundy, Harold. "Justifying Subsecond Response Time." *Computerworld* (Nov. 21, 1983).

Thadhani, A.J. "Interactive User Productivity." *IBM Systems Journal. 20*, 4 (1981).

Thadhani, A.J. "Factors Affecting Programmer Productivity During Development." *IBM Systems Journal 23*, 1 (1984).

"The Economic Value of Rapid Response Time." IBM Form No. GE20-0752 (Nov. 1982). Available through IBM branch office.

PART VII

Productivity Tools

Part VII explains productivity tools used in the Software Factory. Facilitated by 4GLs, prototyping has become a proven concept. Chapter 14 integrates prototyping with the standard System Development Life Cycle (SDLC), clarifying definitions.

Chapter 15 covers hardware, software, and other management techniques. High productivity is a combination of factors, but providing hardware resources (terminals and response time) is a requirement. Other techniques, especially the ability to clone code, are analogous to power tools, a way of speeding up work. Physical location of project teams (a subset of a broader subject of overall working environment) and in-house seminars (a special training technique) are covered.

Two other procedures influencing productivity are formal system test plans and post-implementation audits. Both Chapters 16 and 17 provide actual examples.

In some organizations, the "development center" (a term popularized by IBM) is responsible for researching productivity tools, training, and other administrative support. This separate group assures resources and, more importantly, produces a focal point for addressing productivity in general. However, in our factory, separate groups supported software tools and technical training with line management directly involved in all decisions about productivity tools. Thus, centralizing the development center functions is not imperative.

CHAPTER 14

*Prototyping**

What is a prototype? Such a commonly used term should be easy to define. Test your knowledge by deciding which of the following characterize a prototype:

1. A fourth generation language (4GL) working model that will be rewritten in a procedural language (COBOL, PL1, etc.) for implementation.
2. A quick-and-dirty system intended to be enhanced over time until it is user acceptable.
3. Mock-up of reports (printed) and screens (on-line).
4. All systems implemented with a 4GL.
5. A unique approach that replaces the traditional life cycle for system development.
6. End-user computing.
7. An experiment, similar to research and development, to decide if a system is feasible.
8. A working model with real (live) data.

*Adapted from Johnson, James R. "*A Prototypical Success Story.*" *Datamation* (November 1983) pp. 251–256.

9. A simulation of complex logic in order to determine practicality of the logic.
10. A subset of transactions written in a procedural language.

If you answered yes to all but numbers 4 and 6, you have a fairly clear idea of how prototypes are currently used. Unfortunately, that still leaves room for some confusion. The fact is that some writers have defined prototyping as a complete replacement of the traditional life cycle (TLC), while others view it as a technique to be applied within the TLC. We can resolve this contradiction with a definition that distinguishes among four different levels of prototyping (see Figure 14.1):

Level 1—mock-ups. Output mock-ups of printed reports and/or on-line screens.

Level 2—simulation. Simulated interaction of on-line activity and/or batch reports, with no intent to implement the program or files. Level 2 is used within the TLC during the design phase only. The simulation involves a limited relationship among transactions.

Level 3—working model. A partial system with interaction among files and/or transactions. It has less than complete capabilities in one or all of the functions, transactions, or programs. If completed, part or all of this model could be implemented.

Level 4—research and development. Takes the place of the traditional life cycle approach. Level 4 prototyping is similar to a research project where the result may or may not be pursued. It eliminates the feasibility study and other project phase distinctions.

The first three kinds of prototyping are used in the design phase of the traditional life cycle; the fourth replaces the TLC (see Figure 14.2). For simplicity, assume that the TLC has three phases: feasibility study (general design), detail design, and implementation (where programming is performed). Most organizations have been using level 1 prototyping for a number of years as part of the TLC. It consists of generating mock-up reports and/or screens through print programs or on-line editing tools such as TSO (IBM's Timesharing option). Once created, the output is part of the design documentation. Level 1 prototyping saves prep-

FIGURE 14.1 Relationship of various levels of prototyping to the traditional life cycle.

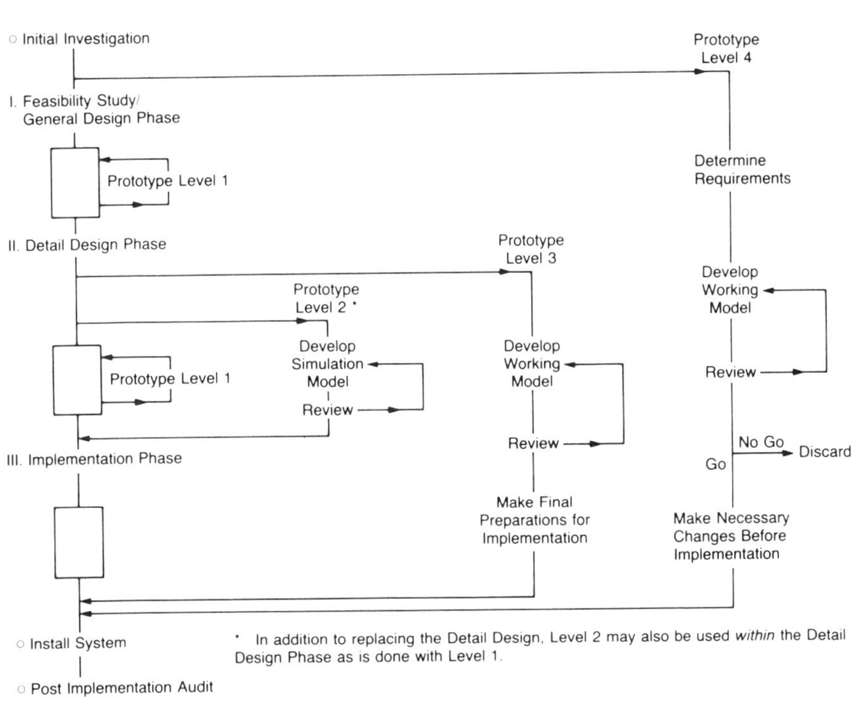

aration effort and is definitely an improvement over typed design documentation.

Level 2 prototyping introduces the concept of simulated interaction of transactions, but with limited relationship among transactions. The programs developed to support the simulation are throwaway—there is no intent to implement the code. A better design results when a user becomes involved with simulated activity; the design process allows for, and is enhanced through, iterations.

In level 3 prototyping, the simulation is replaced with a working model and there is interaction among transactions and files. During this process, the user debugs the design with the working model. Obviously, the model is incomplete when compared to a final implemented system; it is a subset of the final product. However, as distinguished from level 2, part or all of a working model

FIGURE 14.2. Characteristics of the four levels of prototyping.

	Level of Prototyping			
Technique/Characteristic	*1*	*2*	*3*	*4*
1. Mock-up reports/screens	Yes	Yes	Yes	Yes
2. Simulate subset of system functions	No	Yes	Yes	Yes
3. Model system integration and relationships	No	No	Yes	Yes
4. Intend to implement code	No	No	Yes	Yes
5. Use within TLC	Yes	Yes	Yes	No

could be implemented. If the prototype code is eventually put into production, the implementation phase is shortened, because some of the programming has been completed in the design phase.

The general consensus seems to be that levels 2 and 3 are more useful than level 1, and many companies are modifying internal standards to encourage the use of these kinds of prototyping within the traditional system-development life cycle. They minimize design documentation because the simulation or working model serves as the design. One might ask: why not always use level 3—isn't it the natural progression? Not necessarily; consider a system rewrite that changes 25 percent or less of the existing user interface. In this case, level 2 may be the preferred alternative since the user design does not present a major problem. Another factor that dictates a level 2 approach is a high processing volume need where the prototyping language is not suitable for implementation.

BENEFITS HARD TO VISUALIZE

The benefits of some systems are inherently difficult to visualize. Assume, for example, that a manufacturing plant has a batch scheduling system and that a project team is asked to determine the feasibility of a real-time system. In a feasibility study, it is almost impossible to define how a totally different method of operation will affect an entire plant. In this situation, the best way to understand the consequences is to observe a system in operation by implementing a working model. In level 4 prototyping, the model encompasses the feasibility study, the design, and, potentially, the implementation phase; the project phases are merged so that there is no phase distinction. The technique is one of trial and error, and is analogous to a research and development process where a significant percent of the efforts may fail, or lead to a different approach. Conversely, the TLC process sets out to produce a feasible system every time.

As a system development technique that replaces the TLC, level 4 prototyping has the following steps:

- Identify user's basic information requirements.
- Develop working model.
- Use working model to refine needs and justify system.
- Enhance model and possibly implement.

As companies complete the implementation of basic operational systems and proceed to less structured management information systems (MIS), the technique of level 4 prototyping becomes more useful.

No one is happy with the traditional system development life cycle (TLC). Because control was emphasized in the late 1970s, the standards governing the TLC were designed to cover every detail and situation, and ended up becoming overburdening and bureaucratic. Projects that didn't meet users' needs were implemented, and the solution was seen as the addition of design documentation steps that defined those needs more carefully. The specific design tool—whether SDM 70, a problem statement language/analyzer, or PSL/PSA, a structured analysis and design technique—is not relevant. Each technique requires more training and adds more time to the TLC. Thus, it now takes so long to implement a large system that the problem changes during the process, and the design becomes unacceptable.

This is why the TLC has come under attack. But there is hope because the first three levels of prototyping shorten the process, reduce misunderstandings between DP and users, and save time on documentation. In general, prototyping enhances communication because the simulation sessions are more personal and flexible, and are held frequently throughout detail design. The format of such walk-throughs allows for a great deal of discussion. By using prototyping, the users can see versions of the systems early in development to verify their ideas and expectations. When level 2 or 3 prototyping is used, the design document can be more brief since the prototype is part of the design.

Three other criteria not included in the definition are also worth discussing: type of data/files, segmentation, and type of language. Having live data or real files in the simulation is not a requirement, although levels 3 and 4 would generally use live data because it adds realism and facilitates the process.

Segmenting a project—that is, breaking it into smaller, easier-to-manage pieces—is not a definitional criterion for prototyping, but in many cases segmenting is done in conjunction with it.

The type of language is a more controversial criteria to exclude since most illustrations do involve 4GLs. Over a two year period, our organization has worked on numerous level 1 prototypes of all sizes, three level 2 prototypes ranging from two to 20 man-years, five level 3 prototypes ranging from 1 to 50 man-years, and two level 4 prototypes ranging from 5 to 10 man-years. Thus, there have been ten significant projects employing prototyping levels 2 through 4. Six of these projects used 4GL. However, the other four used the standard production language (CICS command level COBOL). One is a level 3 prototype system for a materials warehouse. It is a simplified version of a much more elaborate and costly proposal. If the remaining effort is justified, independent of the initial project, it would be completed as enhancement work. In other words, this project was segmented with the most critical piece first. Since most of the transactions were of medium complexity and since the intent was to implement the prototype, the language of CICS command level COBOL (department standard) was chosen over a 4GL.

We have also built a level 4 prototype, without a 4GL, to define the operational benefits of a real-time manufacturing system. The code generated operated with live data in a test mode for an evaluation period. Final implementations required additional coding to interface to existing systems. All the programs were written in the standard production language (CICS command level COBOL). On both projects, significant manpower time savings resulted from prototyping without a 4GL. But 4GLs do offer a more responsive tool for most prototype situations because of their interpretive nature and nonprocedural code. Because the code is interpretive and does not require a compile, analysts and programmers can perform iterations at a terminal with the user; and the key productivity factor of 4GLs is the automatic features of the high-level coding, the nonprocedural code. However, 4GLs have a significant limitation that is not publicized by the software vendors. This limitation may dictate 4GL production guidelines and may require using the standard language for some level 3 and 4 prototypes.

When a system requires 4GL procedural code because of complexity or special processing, the benefits of the 4GL decrease dramatically. This is because the procedural code of 4GLs, when compared to CICS command level COBOL, is difficult to read, of limited function, symbolic rather than descriptive, and nonstructured. If the programming doesn't require procedural code, a 10 to 1 productivity gain is possible, but as the percent of procedural code increases, the productivity gain is reduced. For example, if a medium-complex 4GL program requires 1,200 statements, a CICS command level COBOL program that performs the same function may need 1,400 statements. If the DP standard is CICS command level COBOL, the minor development gain from writing 200 fewer statements may be lost in the maintenance area.

The solution to this problem is to establish a rule that limits the use of 4GL procedural code in production; our rule is described in Figure 14.3. Only 300 total statements (excluding comments) are allowed. Fifty is the limit for both initialization and processing/data manipulation; simple field validation may be up to 200 statements. These rules are based on the fact that 4GL procedural code is as difficult to write and more difficult to maintain than CICS command level COBOL. Although the rules apply to production, they also influence the selection of prototyping level 2 or 3.

WHICH LEVEL IS RIGHT?

When should prototyping be used, and how do you decide which level is appropriate to the job at hand? An organization

FIGURE 14.3. Procedural code limits for 4GL use.

Function of Procedural Code	*Procedural Code Range*
Initialization	0 to 50
Processing/Data Manipulation	0 to 50
Simple Field Validation	0 to 200
Total combined lines of code	0 to 300 (Plus comments)

Simple validation means field characteristic validation only. Relationship testing and file matching are not regarded as simple in this context. Relationship testing and file matching would be considered processing/ data manipulation.

begins by deciding whether the traditional life cycle should be bypassed in favor of level 4 prototyping.

Providing structure is the inherent reason for the TLC. This structure has a price in documentation, design reviews, approvals, and control. Yet, level 4 does not provide typical control techniques; a project team is free to pursue design in a free-lance mode. Thus, there are disadvantages. Project characteristics favoring a level 4 approach are new technology, innovative software design, and a high degree of uncertainty in the operational impact or benefits, as shown in the real-time manufacturing example.

If the TLC, rather than level 4 prototyping, is chosen as the methodology, proceed to consider which of the other three levels of prototyping might be appropriate. Some level is recommended for every project and, as stated earlier, many corporations have practiced level 1 prototyping for years.

Indeed, the TLC can become bureaucratic, with excessive forms, procedures, and controls. By using either level 2 or 3 prototyping, the TLC can be dramatically accelerated. The factors influencing the selection decision are shown in Figure 5.4.

Both levels 2 and 3 resolve uncertainty during system design. When the project uncertainty is low, a less sophisticated prototype is warranted. Limited innovation may occur on rewrites, existing system enhancements, or smaller projects. As design uncertainty increases, the advantage of a more sophisticated prototype also increases.

FIGURE 14.4. When should prototyping be used?

WHICH LEVEL IS APPROPRIATE?

Traditional Life Cycle vs. **Level 4**

Traditional Life Cycle	vs.	**Level 4**
• Project structure, control, reviews, approvals required *Level 1* • Always used—part of design documentation *Level 2* • Limited innovation and uncertainty • Complex logic or interfaces with other DP systems • Code will not be implemented due to processing constraints or operating standards • Inexperienced users or DP staff *Level 3* • Medium innovation and uncertainty • Simple processing • Few or simple interfaces with other DP systems • Able to implement prototype • Highly experienced user and DP staff		• Project team free to pursue design in a freelance mode • High degree of uncertainty in operational impact or benefits • New technology • Innovative software design • Readily accessible user staff

Directly related to this decision is the ability to implement the code. When it is known that the resulting code will not be implemented because of processing constraints or other operating standards (as may be the case with a 4GL), the level 2 approach is obviously recommended. It would be counterproductive to write a detailed code and then completely rewrite the code. Conversely, by eventually implementing the code as with level 3, productivity is enhanced because less programming is required in the implementation phase.

It is management's responsibility to decide which type of

prototyping applies to an individual project so that the project team will understand the technique and objectives. Prototyping is a philosophy, a new mode of operation. Some resistance may be expected within an organization, but there is no excuse for ignoring this proven concept.

REFERENCES

Boar, Bernard. *Application Prototyping, A Requirements Definition Strategy for the 1980's.* John Wiley & Sons, N.Y. 1984.

Martin, James. *An Information Systems Manifesto.* Prentice Hall, Englewood Cliffs, N.J. 1984.

———. *Application Development without Programmers.* Prentice Hall, Englewood Cliffs, N.J. 1982.

CHAPTER 15

Hardware/Software Tools

This chapter presents six factors directly influencing productivity: terminal availability, batch response time, on-line utility tools, cloning code, project bullpens, and seminars. The first two require adequate hardware, analogous to the concept presented in chapter 1. Selection of utility software products is a priority for all Software Factories. Cloning code, the predecessor of Lower Case (see Chapter 4) improves productivity, especially within project groups. Management support of project bullpens and training seminars also contributes to a productive environment.

TERMINALS

In the past few years, the industry has unanimously acknowledged that a terminal (CRT or PC) is needed for every Software Factory employee. This acknowledgement is based on two factors. First, the majority of activities require access to PC or host data; and second, the price of terminals has dropped considerably. Now, the question is: How many terminals should be provided to each employee? Assuming PCs are not portable, consider the needs and locations:

- The office—where most terminals are today
- Bullpens or labs—a second work area
- Home—a common workplace for electronic mail and other activities
- Travel—a portable for word processing and electronic mail

Justifying three or four terminals per person is an adventure today, but, in a few years, the ratio of 3:1 will be realistic. In our factory, loaner home terminals are provided upon request, primarily for solving production problems during implementations. As prices drop, additional terminals for bullpens (comparable to labs) will be justified.

Other secondary issues concerning terminals are 132 characters and system windowing. A 132-character CRT allows easy on-line viewing of traditional 132-character reports, and allows more data (file record data in particular) to be displayed on the screen.

System windowing allows a terminal to be signed on to multiple systems (TSO, CICS, production, etc.) concurrently. Windowing or split-screen capability allows viewing and activity against all systems.

QUICK BATCH RESPONSE TIME

While most of the computer tasks are on-line, there are still some functions that must be done in batch mode. Batch turnaround includes getting the jobs executed quickly and delivering any printed output without delay.

Endorsing the value of short queue time, service-level agreements with the data center provide a maximum of 5 minutes execution queue time for 90 percent of priority jobs, and a maximum of 10 minutes queue time for 90 percent of nonpriority jobs. But, in the factory, achieving quick turnaround has been a priority and, as a result, service-level agreements have been exceeded—the average queue time for all tests is less than three minutes and, for high priority tests, it is less than one minute!

Also, as a part of quick turnaround, the data center delivers printed output at half-hour intervals. Faster delivery is desired, but the inefficiency of stopping the high-speed laser printers more frequently to remove printed output makes this impractical.

ON-LINE SOFTWARE UTILITY TOOLS

Ranging from test data generators to sophisticated on-line hex and dump analysis calculators to on-line debugging software and utilities make the staff's jobs quicker and easier.

Most of these are on-line tools accessible through a user menu. The menu illustrated in Figure 15.1 provides access to 64 different on-line tools. The two screens making up this menu suggest the capabilities. Improving and adding to the tools available is a high priority.

CLONING CODE

Several years ago, software was developed that built skeleton COBOL modules based on input parameters. After using it and cloning techniques in similar situations, the staff preferred cloning, i.e., starting with an existing program and changing it for their needs. Today, the practice of "cloning" code has permeated the organization and, in some cases, reusable code has been developed.

Many projects involve major enhancements or additions to existing systems. Often, when starting to write a new batch program or on-line transaction in this environment, the programmer/analyst will use an existing program with at least some similar functions as a basis for cloning. In some cases, this existing program may serve only as a skeleton, with a few I/O routines that can be used and, perhaps, some data division items. But in other cases, this existing program may have much code that can be used, such as complex file navigation code, screen layouts and logic, and table maintenance.

When project groups have functions or routines that are used frequently, reusable modules are created. The number of modules created is limited but, when used, it is an important technique. As an example, one large on-line application system has a reusable code library of about 7,000 lines of code (LOC) which represents

FIGURE 15.1. Programmer's tool menu.

```
__________ FOREGROUND (ON-LINE) PROCESSING __________PAGE 1 SELECT
OPTION →

 1) JES SPOOL DISPLAY/SEARCH         2) MISCELLANEOUS BROWSE
 3) DATA TRANSMISSION FACILITY       4) TEXT LIBRARIAN PROCESSING
 5) UTPGM                            6) LIBRARIAN PROCESSING
 7) OUTLIST-DISPLAY HELD OUTPUT      8) OLD COBOL COMPILE
 9) OLD ASSEMBLY/LINK EDIT          10) COBOL COMPILE (CENTRIC)
11) SORTWORK CALCULATOR             12) CICS PROCESSING
13) RDS BROWSE/MAINTENANCE          14) ASSEMBLY/LINK EDIT
15) MOMS (SPF VERSION)              16) TSOCAT (CATALOG LOOKUP)
17) LOAD PDS DIRECTORY INFO         18) DGA
19) MSS SPACE CALCULATION           20) EDIT MACRO LIBRARY
21) SCHED. MAIN. (COORD ONLY)       22) TEST DATASET SCRATCH/ARCHIVE
23) CICS TRANSACTION DUMPS          24) OLD CICS MAP/COPYLIB ASM
25) INFORMATION MVS                 26) MASTER OPERATOR JOB SUBMIT
27) INFOJCL-PROD. JCL BROWSE        28) SPACE MANAGEMENT SYSTEM
29) VSAM                            30) CICS HELP COPY/UPDATE
31) COBOL DEBUG FACILITY            32) PROGRAM CROSS REFERENCE
33) SORT FACILITY                   34) OLD CICS ONLINE COMPILE
35) PRODUCTION RUNBOOKS             36) PL/1 COMPILE

        (*** PRESS ENTER FOR PAGE 2 OR END TO TERMINATE ***)
```

```
__________ FOREGROUND (ON-LINE) PROCESSING ________________PAGE 2
SELECT OPTION →

37) DA—DISPLAY ACTIVE JOBS          38) DN—DISPLAY JOB STATUS
39) SDATE PROMPTER                  40) COPY W/INCLUDE/EXCLUDE/CHANGE
41) JCL BUILD/VERIFY/BUILD GDG      42) RDS BROWSE/ALTER RDS INFO
43) APG AUTO PROGRAM GENERATOR      44) PROGRAMMER NUMBER LOOKUP
45) SOURCE FILE COMPARISON          46) BMS MACRO GENERATOR
47) STANDARD ABBREVIATIONS          48) LEXICON SCAN
49) DAILY INFO JCL                  50) IEBCOPY FROM PDS DIRECTORY
51) JOB STREAM/PROC GENERATOR       52) JCL RESTART DECK GENERATOR
53) PRINTOFF                        54) ONLINE MARKIV FACILITY
55) LEXICON CROSS REFERENCE         56) MASS STORAGE MOUNT
57) "AFP" JCL CONVERSION AID        58) MULTI JOB RELEASE/PURGE
59) DEFAULT JOB CARD ACCT INFO      60) TCT CONFIGURATION DATA BASE
61) "OLD" COMPILE/LINK              62) DC—DISPLAY CENTRIC STATUS
63) BATCH TERMINAL FACILITY         64) RESERVED FOR NEW LEXICON
65) DGAISPF-SPLIT SCREEN

   (*** PRESS END KEY FOR PAGE 1 OR RETURN KEY TO TERMINATE ***)
```

FIGURE 15.2. Training architecture.

Type	*Description*	*Objective*
I. MIS		
A. Department	Sessions to review division activities	Informational/ consistency
B. Seminars		
1) Discussion sessions	Discussion of topics related to work methods	To share ideas methods, and techniques
2) Information sessions	General update on work related topics	Provide info on directions, plans, projects
3) Update sessions	Presentation of specific techniques, tools, methods	Awareness of facilities and how to use them
C. Training Classes	Formal training by MIS Training	Educational
II. Corporate		
A. Corporate Training	Formal training by corp. training; usually motivational or management	Educational
III. External		
A. Management	Noncorporate supplied training/exposure to management	Educational
B. Application	Business function training, usually supplied with purchased product	Educational
C. Technical	Technical, by commercial companies	Educational

only two percent of the code written for the project but, with multiple uses within the system, it accounts for more than 10 percent of the total LOC.

PROJECT BULLPENS

Years ago, after all staff members had been given their own terminals, the project work area "bullpens" (a traditional part of our work environment) disappeared quickly as most project groups chose to put terminals in the offices. However, after a period of time, some groups asked for bullpens again. While people enjoyed the privacy and lack of disturbances in their offices, they also found that they were much less aware of what the rest of the project group was doing. For groups working on one common project, a bullpen is recommended. During a systems test phase, in particular, the better group communications associated with the bullpen can help productivity.

SEMINARS

Various types of training have different objectives: a corporate training class might focus on leadership or general management, other technical training is specific to a product or software package. The training "architecture" is shown in Figure 15.2. The seminar training approach fills an important niche in a professional environment. It allows peers to exchange ideas, discuss management direction, and learn about beneficial techniques.

Examples of seminars conducted for project managers are:

Project Management
Joint Application Design (JAD)
End User Computing
PC Communication

Approximately 30 individuals attend each one-to-two hour session.

REFERENCES

McDonald, James. "Maximizing Systems Development Productivity," *Systems Development*, 7, 10, (Oct. 1987).

CHAPTER 16

Test Plans

Success and quality of a project implementation is directly related to the system test plan. For critical projects, a formal written plan is a requirement. This is true with or without a quality control organization. In our factory, the project team was responsible for quality control since a separate organization did not exist. In this chapter, after defining four levels of testing, brief instructions state the contents of a system test plan. Excerpts from an Accounts Payable rewrite project provide an example.

In the Software Factory, four primary testing levels were defined: unit, integration, system, and user acceptance. Other test plans, such as disaster recovery or volume tests, were performed as needed. The following definitions explain the primary tests.

- Unit. Testing of all logic paths in the programs with generated or production data to ensure correctness of individual programs.
- Integration. Coordinated testing of multiple programs with generated or production data. The purpose is to ensure program correctness of a related group of programs within a system.
- System. Execution of the system in a "production-like" environment to ensure that the system operates properly from both program and procedural standpoints.

- User Acceptance. Ensures that the user understands the system's operational requirements, capabilities, and deliverables. Normally, users will participate in planning and testing as well as inputting test data and reviewing the results. The user acceptance test may be part of the system test.

TEST PLAN ORGANIZATION AND EXAMPLE

The written test plan includes an Overview, a Test Plan Procedure, Test Plan Details, Conversion Plan, and an Appendix for detail. The example follows each instruction.

I. The Overview

Purpose. Brief outline of the types of testing to be performed and responsibilities of user and MIS personnel.

Example

This document describes the tests that will be conducted prior to installation of the Accounts Payable Payee Rewrite Project. The test environment will be similar to the production environment to ensure: the proper functioning of all Accounts Payable programs, the proper functioning of all interfaces with other systems, and user understanding and acceptance of the system.

Outline of the specific objectives of the testing, including items such as the following: specific responsibilities of all departments and individuals; description of time commitments required of users for data preparation, data entry, and analysis of output; outline of unusual requirements for technical or environmental requirements; and schedule for the testing process.

The testing required to install the new Payee on-line system for Accounts Payable (AP) will be done in five cycles covering daily, weekly, month-end, and day after month-end conditions; plus a start-up cycle to convert files to the new formats and prepare files for use in cycle 1. In addition, each cycle will create test files for use by those systems that interface with Accounts Payable.

System testing will be conducted by the AP project group. The users will prepare and input all on-line test data, and will review all on-line screens and all batch output to verify that the system is functioning properly. The AP project group will submit all batch jobs and verify file content.

Testing of year-end processing is not included in this plan. A separate test will be conducted before year-end 1988 covering year-end programming changes.

Time will be allotted to run all five cycles three times, although the third set of cycles may not be needed. In addition to the above cycles, an acceptance test will be run using full production files and standalone tests will be run of the quarterly and request jobs.

The system test Gantt chart is shown in Appendix A (not included). It contains projected start-up of all testing.

II. Test Plan Procedure

The primary objective of this section is to document a logical plan for executing testing cycles.

Example

The pre-cycle is the startup cycle. The existing system test master files (which were originally extracted from production files) will be used. The record layouts of some of these master files will change, and these files will be converted to their new formats. Then a portion of the daily batch pass will be run to create on-line files for start-up of cycle 1.

Cycles 1 through 4 form the bulk of the system test. The input for these cycles is prepared and input by the user to test the various paths of the system. These tests will ensure that all on-line processing and the nightly batch processing for daily, weekly, and month-end are functioning correctly.

Cycle 5 tests the batch pass only (no on-line input). It will ensure that the month-end files wrap correctly and that the system can process without any input.

III. Details of the Test Plan

The level of detail may vary considerably from one system to another. In all cases, however, the basic format of "test case" followed by "expected results" is to be observed. Break down a testing level into "cycles" of testing such as a daily cycle, a weekly cycle, a monthly, and so on. Each cycle is then divided into "steps" made up of test cases and expected results. Showing the name of the individual assigned to specific tests may also be appropriate. The conditions to be tested for each step are usually placed in an appendix.

Example

This project originated because of the need to upgrade the payee on-line system. The most significant change was the expansion and reorganization of the payee numbering structure. Since this payee number is used extensively throughout the AP system, most existing programs, both batch and on-line, required changes.

This system test will cover not only the rewritten on-line Payee subsystem, but also the revised Invoice, Purchase Order, Receiving Match, and Check Writing on-line subsystems. All batch programs that execute daily, weekly and monthly will be included in the testing.

The pre-cycle is used to prepare the on-line files for use by the user to input transactions for cycle 1. The Payee Master, Freight Reference, Invoice Master, Invoice History, and Purchase Order files will be converted to their new record formats. A portion of the batch pass will be run to create other files that are needed by the on-line system, such as the Invoice Paging, Invoice Key, and Open Vendor files.

Cycle 1 is a daily pass. All AP programs that execute daily will be tested. The user will input on-line transactions, and these transactions will be run through the daily batch pass. The user and the AP project group will check out all daily reports created in this pass.

Cycle 2 is a second daily pass. All AP programs that execute daily will be tested. The user will input on-line transactions, and these transactions will be run through the daily batch pass. The user and the AP project group will check out reports created in this pass. Although cycles 1 and 2 are both daily-only passes, different conditions are tested in each cycle.

Cycle 3 is a weekend pass. All AP programs that execute daily and weekly will be tested. Again, the user will input on-line transactions, and these transactions will be run through the daily and weekly batch pass. The user and the AP project group will check out all reports created in this pass.

Cycle 4 is a month-end pass. All AP programs that execute daily, weekly, and monthly will be tested in the same manner as the above cycles. The batch pass will create daily, weekly, and monthly reports for checkout by the user and the AP project group.

Cycle 5 is a day-after-month-end pass. This cycle has no online input, but again produces daily reports for user and AP project group checkout. This cycle is used to ensure that all files are wrapping correctly after a month-end pass, and that the system can execute with no on-line input. See Appendix C (not included) for a matrix of procedures to be tested in each cycle.

The testing of quarterly jobs and request jobs will be conducted as standalone tests. The reports produced will be verified by both the user and the AP project group.

Each cycle will create files for use by those systems that interface with the AP system. The AP project group will furnish those files to the interfacing project group for use in their testing. See Appendix D (not included) for a list of interface files.

The Accounts Payable Manager will prepare all on-line input. He or she will make certain that there are transactions included to test all portions of the on-line and batch systems thoroughly. See Appendix E (not included) for a list of conditions to be tested.

IV. Conversion Plan

This section lists the files (databases) and processing required for conversion.

Example:

Convert the following files:

Payee Master
Freight Reference
Invoice Master

Invoice History
Purchase Order

Create the following new files:

Payee Character
Payee Phonetic
Payee Pick
Payee Tax ID Number

A memo will be distributed before the installation date detailing the timing of implementation of changes in other systems that interface with Accounts Payable.

V. Appendix

Include items such as: System Test Gantt Chart, Problem Point Sheet, Matrix of Procedures to Be Tested, Interface Files, and Conditions to Be Tested. Excerpts from the last item are included in the example.

Examples:

On-line Processing Conditions to Be Tested

AP24 - Add/Chg/Inq Freight Invoice. Screen changed: payee number, zip code and corporation code expanded, payee summary field deleted, function eight (payee summary list) added, corporation code and payee terms rearranged, payee number and name reversed. Test function one (add/return). Test function two (inquire on invoice). Test function three (change/return). Test function four (reject invoice). Test function five (delete invoice). Test function eight (payee summary list). New function to transfer to the new payee subsystem.

Batch Processing Conditions to Be Tested

Ensure that the following reports are created to verify that the expanded corporation code and payee numbers are being handled properly by the following transactions: AP010, PA254, AP185, AP186, AP106.

CHAPTER 17

Post-Implementation Audits

Post-implementation audits provide a database to assess productivity tools and project management techniques. About half of the projects completed receive an audit by "internal" personnel, those employed by the Software Factory versus external auditors. Performing an audit provides important training to the auditor: first, there is exposure to a new application since the individual selected for the audit was not part of the project team; second, the auditor has the opportunity to study the complete Systems Development life cycle; and last, auditing requires a thorough review of project management standards.

If audits are not conducted, consider this management technique as a productivity tool. Its impact on improving productivity is impossible to measure, but subjective feeling classifies the process as an important tool. Instructions for performing a post-implementation audit are followed by excerpts from an actual audit.

I. GENERAL DESCRIPTION

Briefly describe the project and include purpose, requestor, expected benefits, size and scope, and relationship to other major projects.

Example

The Everyday Stock Number File On-line project was part of an overall effort to give inventory controllers, analysts, and other personnel on-line access and update to the Everyday files. The Inventory Controllers expect to save $500,000 per year from improved serviceability. The project consists of 11 new CICS programs, 8 new batch programs, 35 new procedures, changes to 18 existing procedures, and 4 changes to existing programs.

II. GENERAL COMMENTS

Overall Comments

State the most significant factors contributing to the success or failure of the project. The auditor should seek candid comments from project team members to help with the evaluation and must not be reluctant to include critical or complimentary comments when justified.

Example

The Everyday Stock Number File On-line project is an example of how a project should work. The users were involved with the design and implementation of the project, resulting in a smooth implementation ahead of schedule, with no significant changes requested after implementation. No significant problems were encountered during the implementation of the project. The project was installed three months ahead of schedule.

Problems

Describe any significant design, programming, or implementation/conversion problems. Did any of the problems require changes to the development schedule or increase the effort significantly? Were all requested changes adequately handled by the change control procedures? Were all design requirements completed, or were some scheduled as enhancements?

Example

The original plan to make the stock number file a real-time on-line system could not be accomplished (at a reasonable cost), due to interface problems with the batch Everyday system. Instead, an on-line validation with batch update was implemented. All design requirements were completed as part of the original project. Enhancements were minor and incorporated without change control documents.

Successful Techniques

Describe any new or existing techniques that were particularly successful. Were any variations of the existing development standards proven successful enough that the standard should be changed?

Example

The same users (inventory controllers) were consulted as transactions were prototyped. This continuity developed user familiarity with the transactions, improving the quality of the final product and increasing the user enthusiasm.

A library of standard common code was set up by project members. This code was used in each new program, speeding the original coding of the programs and making maintenance of the system easier in the future. Weekly walk-throughs of programs were conducted by project members. This improved communication within the project group and decreased mistakes and task overlap due to misunderstanding.

User training paralleled production system without actual production data. By using a realistic training plan, users could concentrate on learning the new transactions, rather than pointing out the inconsistencies between the training system and the "real" system. Extensive help screens were developed by the project group, easing the transition to the new system and reducing the number of user phone calls after installation.

User Involvement

Describe the extent to which users were involved in each phase of the project. Were user personnel assigned specifically to this project?

Example

The users were very involved in all phases of the project. A major portion of the success of this project was user enthusiasm and interaction with the project group. Minor problems in the design of some screens can be traced to some users not reviewing the prototype screens at an early phase of development. Specific users were assigned to test the programs and continued with the project until installation.

Other

Comment on the following topics when appropriate: Was an adequate effort made tuning programs? Was hard copy output avoided when possible, and was the technique of exception-reporting used when appropriate? Was the purchase of proprietary software adequately evaluated as an alternative? Were Warnier diagrams of program logic completed in the design phase or the implementation phase or both?

Example

The Stock Number On-Line group designed an effective system with efficient programs. Hard copy output was avoided when possible, and the technique of exception-reporting was used when appropriate. Warnier diagrams of program logic were completed in the implementation phase of the project.

III. DEVELOPMENT AND INSTALLATION STANDARDS

Comment on the extent the development and installation standards were followed. Was appropriate authorization received and documented in cases where the standards were not followed?

Example

No feasibility study or general design was done, since the design was replaced by level 2 prototyping. All aspects of the Project Control Standard for Large Projects were successfully met.

The Systems Development documentation package was complete and well organized in its own binder. The user documentation standards were satisfied by the on-line help screens and a printed system narrative. The Data Center Operations documentation was complete according to standards.

IV. ACTUAL VERSUS ESTIMATES

Comment on the comparison of key estimates to actual results. If there were significant variances, explain the reasons.

Example

The project was originally estimated at 600 man-days but actually took 435 man-days to complete. Project members attribute the 165 day difference to: test plan generator, similarity of some on-line programs, and the group's ability to clone code from previously written programs, reduced system test time based on limited system interactions, and some possible overestimating.

V. LINES OF CODE

The purpose of this section is to document the actual lines of code (LOC) counts necessary to compute lines of code rates. Only lines of code in implemented production programs should be counted. Complete lines of code counts and the computed lines of code rates per separate instruction. Comment on the comparison of the total lines of code rate to average rates. If there is a significant difference, explain the reasons for the difference.

Example

All projects average 75.1 lines of code per man-day with a range of 32.2–147.0 LOC per day. This project averaged 124.4

lines of code per man-day, a figure at the upper end of the acceptable range. Most of this deviation can be attributed to the high percentage of new code written in this project.

VI. PRODUCTION SYSTEM PERFORMANCE

Comment on how well the installed system has performed in the production environment. Include comments on the following questions: Did the users find the system easy to use? Were the users satisfied with the system's capabilities? Have many enhancements been requested? Has Systems Development been able to support the system easily? Has the Data Center been able to meet the production schedule? How many UCRs were written during the first three months after installation?

Example

The installed system has performed very well in production, with only three Unusual Condition Reports (UCRs) written during the first three months after installation. The users find the system easy to use and are satisfied with its capabilities. The minor enhancements requested have been installed for less than five man-days.

VII. USER ACCEPTANCE COMMENTS

Offer the users the opportunity to submit written comments on acceptance of the system. Summarize these comments into the audit report in this section and include specific detail comments as attachments.

Example

The users have been quite pleased with the project. They felt that the number of reviews during implementation was adequate and that few problems were encountered. One user mentioned that he had seen few projects go any better.

Part VIII

Managing the Utility

The modern data center is viewed as a utility, a service providing computer resources with high availability and low response time—common functions like water and electric utilities.

Defining and monitoring utilities' Critical Success Factors (CSF) is an important management function. Reports written by Data Center personnel with end-user software, can monitor progress toward these objectives.

Two required systems, problem reporting and change control, provide sources for data extract, dramatically reducing manual reporting. Periodic meetings communicate information among vendors, technical staff, network group, and operations. Productivity measures and a recommended course of action are also discussed in chapter eighteen.

CHAPTER **18**

*Managing the Utility**

This chapter documents the results of a project to define Data Center Critical Success Factors (CSF). Hopefully, readers will be able to apply one or more ideas expressed, either specific reports or management philosophy toward meetings, change control, and daily discussions.

The Data Center provides a computing utility. It includes 108 personnel allocated as:

Data Center	
Operations	64
Network	8
Admin. Svcs.	16
Data Input	20

The four operations shifts are on a 3 day 12 hour work week. Each shift has 10 operators, 5 analysts and one manager. The Data Center organization is responsible for production passes,

*Adapted from Johnson, James R. "Operation Productivity Standards and Statistics." *Data Center Operations Management* (New York: Auerbach Publishers, @ 1990 Warren Gorham & Lamont Inc.).

Network Help Desk, first and second line communication support, and Data Center hardware. Another technical group installed system software. The operations staff of 64 personnel supports: 65,000 batch jobs per month, 8 million feet of printed paper per month, and 100,000 tape mounts per month.

The hardware includes the following:

One IBM 3090 600E
One Amdahl 5990 1400
460 GBYTES of IBM and NAS disk
Three IBM 3800 printers
Three microfilm cameras
2700 terminals (76% local)
1000 PCs

The following question and answer dialog explains the management of the computer utility.

Question: *How do you manage the Data Center?*

Response: A variety of management techniques are used to manage the Data Center. In addition to the Corporate Budget process, administrative reports are prepared monthly. Also, a yearly planning meeting establises a work plan with To-Dos scheduled during the year.

Question: *Do you have other performance and production reports?*

Response: Yes, the Technical Service Group produces a number of performance reports covering: resource utilization (CPU, disk, tape), TSO and CICS response time, network availability, and system through-put for both batch and on-line. On the production side, the Console/Network Analyst utilizing basic End User tools, produces a series of daily and monthly reports for monitoring critical success factors. A standards and statistics report published monthly and summarized annually identifies exceptions and monitors trends.

Question: *How are problems communicated and resolved?*

Response: Communications is accomplished through MIS meetings and also meetings with vendors. Two applications aid the process. The first, a preventive system called Change Control, documents system and major changes in advance. The second is Problem Management, a means of recording errors, assigning responsibility and following up on the disposition/resolution. Both of these systems are real time.

Question: *What are critical production activities monitored daily?*

Response: The Problem Management System logs all problems as they occur. Major problems are reported in four production reports reviewed each morning by the Vice President of MIS and hs management team.

Question: *You mean the staff meets every morning?*

Response: Yes, for 15 to 30 minutes, five days a week. General management issues are discusssed along with the reports containing monitored activities such as: pass completions, reasons for late passes, unusual system occurrences, and network status.

Question: *Will you explain each of these?*

Response: An extract of the Pass Completions report is shown in Figure 18.1. It lists scheduled/actual completion times for critical passes, on-lin files (shown), and reports. The 28 items on the complete report define the critical corporate activities. The asterisk on the "EVDAY" system indicates a delay explained on the next report, Reasons for Late Passes, shown in Figure 18.2. In this particular situation the Unusual Condition Report (UCR) was not a program bug, but rather due to a business distribution problem (high volume of backorders). Causes of late passes are summarized monthly. Other significant problems emerge on the next report, Unusual System Occurrences. As Figure 18.3 states on December 7, the "IBM 3090" system went into error recovery. Communicating network problems is the purpose of the last report, Network Daily Status, shown in Figure 18.4. On the particular day there were no CICS or Data Base problems, However, one modem failed resulting in 22 minutes of down time on one line.

All of the four reports include manual input from the Console/Network Analyst. The data is entered on-line requiring only 10–15 minutes per day. The report shell is produced by TSO and SAS "programming".

Question: *How does change control work?*

Response: Changes to the operating system, database utilities, CICS, and major batch systems are defined in advance via the online Change Control System. Each week a list of future activity is printed in date sequence. Figure 18.5 illustrates an example of three different changes with severity noted in the S/T (severity type) column. Severity type one, an operating system fix, has the potential for the greatest adverse impact versus a severity three which may only impact a portion of the system. Note the descriptions in Figure 18.5 are not necessarily self-explanatory, but written for those familiar with the change.

Question: *Who attends the meeting and what action can they make?*

Response: The Change Control meeting is a management meeting including all those reporting to the Vice President. Their review focuses on the number of severity level ones and twos occurring on the same weekend. They have the authority to delay changes or resolve conflicts. However, the value of this management meeting is not measured by the number of delays, rather, it assures management commitment and involvement with change control. Other tactical meetings provide personnel with more specific coordination information.

Question: *Who attends these other meetings?*

Response: The groups communicating in support of change control are: Vendors, Operations, Network Staff, and Technical Services. Three meetings take place: one on Hardware chaired by Operations, one on the Network, chaired by Technical Services, and one on Communications chaired by the Network Staff.

Question: *How do you force people, say vendors, to attend?*

Response: This hasn't been a problem because of the meeting procedure, for example:

Date and time fixed
Same attendees
Notes published next day
Standard distribution
Attendance noted

In multivendor shops, vendors appreciate information on changes planned. In these meetings problems are also discussed.

Question: *What other statistics are reported?*

Response: Monthly and Yearly causes for late passes are documented and compared (Ref Figure 18.6). Also, volume statistics are plotted for batch jobs, reruns, microfilm output, reports printed. For example the current rerun percent was .2 (1800 reruns divided by 806,000 jobs). Initial program loads (IPLs) comparisons receive considerable attention. Two types of IPLs exist, planned and unplanned. The latter cause unscheduled downtime. As with most MIS shops, vast reductions in both types of IPLs has occurred over the years. One month a few years ago, our two main computers experienced 28 IPLs (12 planned and 16 unplanned). The recent monthly average was three (2 planned and 1 unplanned). Although average restart time dropped from 97 minutes to 88 minutes, an automated IPL system will soon produce more dramatic reductions. The goal is 15–20 minutes.

Other Network Status Reports (example not included) show the percent availability, reasons for non-availability, and average restart time. Data for each of the eight CICS regions (plus eight for test) and the two data base regions (plus two for test) are reported.

Question: *Is hardware maintenance monitored?*

Response: Yes, two reports are created from the UCR system. The first is for Computer Room Hardware. It lists each device, the number of failures and time to fix, for example;

	Total Number of Devices	Number of Failures	Hours Device Down	Comments
DASD 3800	122	1	4	Head Disk Assembly (HDA) replaced

The problem was due to a head crash which subsequently distributed fine metal particles through-out the box. Fortunately, the critical data sets were copied prior to complete failure, and also a replacement HDA was locally available reducing the down time.

Another report lists failures associated with devices outside of the Data Center, such as printers, CRTs, CPU, etc. Exception conditions are noted.

Question: *Are staff errors monitored?*

Response: Yes, the Problem Management System records all errors assigning a cause code to each one, occasionally belatedly since the cause may not be known when the error occurs. Unusual conditions are reported by each department within MIS including the Data Center. Associated with each error is delay time, the item to correct the problem (time from abend to restart). For Data Center personnel, Figure 18.7 shows the Year End Totals. Columns were produced for each of the four shifts with the results circulated to all. Obviously, peer pressure existed to reduce delay time and substantial improvement resulted—from 65 hours in the previous year to 21 hours in the current year.

Question: *Do UCRs influence pay or performance reviews?*

Response: Reducing UCRs is both a department and individual objective so it can be part of a performance review which in turn impacts pay. However, managers use their own discretion, no policy exists.

Question: *Were all the reports created by Data Center personnel?*

Response: Yes, but remember two applications systems, Change Control and Problem Management, exist, thus data can be extracted for reports. End User tools, primarily SAS and TSO, were used. The systems minimize the time to obtain the information, however, many different areas feed the two systems.

Question: *Have you devloped productivity measures for the Data Center?*

Response: Yes, but we had to modify them considerably recently. The first calculations included five outputs: number of tape mounts, feet of paper printed, number of microfilm frames, reports delivered, and batch jobs run. To calculate productivity each of these outputs was divided by the resource required. For example (monthly figures):

$$P = \frac{O}{R} = \frac{13{,}336{,}352 \text{ (frames of microfilm)}}{6{,}480 \text{ (operator hours)}}$$

But what happens, as in our situation, when a project to reduce the quantity of microfilm is successful? Productivity goes down! Now in the long run, if output reductions exceeded say 25%, staff reductions would result and productivity would rise. But these changes may take years. Also consider paper reports, most data centers are striving for remote printing—an objective which also lowers the productivity unless the majority of reports are distributed. The same can be true for tapes, if a project to move frequently mounted tapes and other temporary files to disk is successful. Reference Figure 18.8 for an example of how our productivity measure varied from month to month. Thus, calculations require constant review and modification to reflect actual productivity. One approach is more sophistication entailing more complexity, a non-desirable option. Another approach is simplicity, such as selecting one output for the entire Data Center. This was our option. The choice was the number of batch jobs, an output growing at a steady rate. Volume of on-line transactions is another option. The primary purpose of productivity calculations is not to design a perfect measure with associated bureaucracy but rather to focus attention on productivity.

Question: How does Automated Operation impact your monitoring activities.

Response: The term Automated Operations is an umbrella term covering all aspects of Data Center management. However, various automation tools should improve the critical factors monitored, such as, pass completions, network status, number of reruns, number of IPLs, network availability, and staff errors.

Recommended Course of Action

Data Center managers should periodically review existing reports and procedures, questioning their value. This chapter explained our organization's Data Center critical success factors. Emphasis was on the following:

Production Passes—	Does a checkpoint system exist for critical batch passes? Are reasons for delays recorded and given visibility?
File Availability—	Does a checkpoint system exist for critical and online files? Are reasons for delays recorded and given visibility?
Unusual Conditions—	Does management review all major unusual contitions daily? Is history maintained, analyzed?
Network Failures—	Is each network failure with its associated down time recorded and routed to management?
Maintenance—	Are statistics updated on vendor maintenance service, data such as, time to fix and service required by machine type?
Change Control—	Are all maintenace changes, both hardware and software, approved in advance by a change control committee? Does staff have the opportunity to review planned and approved changes?
Individual Errors—	Is each department and manager held responsible for errors caused by personnel in their group? Are controllable (delay time) errors separated from uncontrollable?
Performance Measures—	Are performance measures published for end user availability and restart time?

Do these critical success factors apply in your company? If so, the Data Center staff can utilize end user programming tools to produce similar monitoring reports.

FIGURE 18.1 Pass completions.

Daily Passes Online Files Available

Compl	*Sched*	*System*	*Job*
0005	0300	Employee Info	EIDPR270
0403	0530	Graphic Arts	PMDGT050
*0752	0630	EVDAY	EVDMH630
0548	0700	Pre-Production	PPDDE270

FIGURE 18.2 Reasons for late passes.

UCR #	Late Pass	Lost Time	Reason
89025032	EVDAY	0	Job normally runs an average of 30 minutes. It ran 1 and 45 minutes tonight. It was adding 17000 back orders to the release processing.

FIGURE 18.3 Unusual system occurrences.

Date	Time	System	Description
12/06	0700		No problems to report on nights.
12/07	0600	S284	IBM 3090 went into error recovery—Bad TCM. After talking to IBM support in Atlanta we initialized the system.

FIGURE 18.4 Network daily status.

CICS/DB Failures

Region	Time Down	Time Up	Related UCR#	Problem/ Resolution
			No Problems to Report	

Circuit/Hardware Failures

Device	Time Down	Time Up	Related UCR#	Problem/ Resolution
LW1/LW2	2010	2032	89032013	Intermittent hits on devices. Moved lines to spare modem. Moved lines back after modem was verified by vendor.

FIGURE 18.5 Change control input.

Trgt Date	*Comp Date*	*S T*	*Mgrs*	*Num*	*Area Impacted*	*Description of Change*
12/17	12/17	2	AC/PT	1113	KC-------	Installation of Online Insurance System
12/18	12/17	1	JM/MM	1185	KC-ENF-LIB	IBM 3090 Apply program fix (UY24818) to correct problem vary path function.
01/29	01/29	3	JJ/WG	1177	KC-------	Initialize all CRT control control units before leaving Saturday night. This will make us aware of any reader or diskette problem. If any problem, create UCR for Sunday IBM CE.

FIGURE 18.6 Causes for late passes.

	1989	*1988*	*1987*
DataBase	17	17	60
Elapsed Time	63	40	34
Hardware	4	10	25
Program	99	45	60
Operations	1	4	5
Software	3	1	3
Other	14	19	29
TOTAL	201	136	216

FIGURE 18.7 UCRs for data center personnel.

Cause Codes	*Year End Totals 1989* #	*DT*	*LT*
Data Center Computer Operator Error	30	4.9	2.7
Microfilm Operator	10	0	7.4
Data Center Analyst Error	124	12.2	.5
Reports Distributor Error	51	3.7	.3
Other	13	5.0	2.1
TOTAL	216	20.8	13.6

\# Number of UCRs
DT Delay Time
Elapsed Time From Abend to Restart (hours, minutes)
LT Lost Time
Elapsed Processing Time to Abend (hours, minutes)

FIGURE 18.8. Productivity measures.

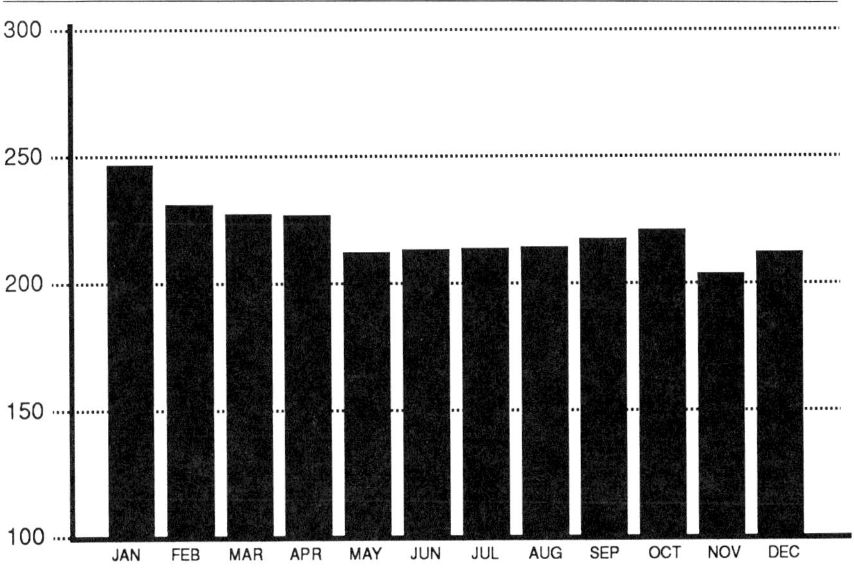

Appendix A

Factory Statistics

	LOC REPORT								*REPORTED FOR PROJECT*					
	LOC				*PGMS*									
	O/L	*BAT*	*TOT (Mil)*	*LOC ADDED (Mil)*	*O/L*	*BATCH*	*TOTAL*	*ADDED PGMS*	*TOT IMP*	*PROJ LATE*	*OVER BUDG*	*IMP UCRs*	*MD ON PROJ*	*LOC (Mil)*
	A	*B*	*C*	*D*	*E*	*F*	*G*	*H*	*I*	*J*	*K*	*L*	*M*	*N*
1982	—	—	5.7	1.5	—	—	5,137	—	48	—	—	390	22,565	1.52
1983	1.7	6.0	7.7	2.0	835	5,304	6,139	1,002	41	—	—	332	18,824	1.6
1984	2	6.7	8.8	1.0[1]	1,034	5,643	6,677	538	45	8	13	282	13,503	1.33
1985	3	7.7	10.7	1.9	1,258	6,259	7,517	840	51	12	15	391	21,374	2.38
1986	4.5	7.7	12.2	1.5	1,658	6,284	7,942	425	57	4	8	338	16,583	1.86
1987	5.6	8.3	13.9	2.0[2]	1,032	2,477	3,509[3]	—	42	6	11	297	16,252	2.37
1988	6.3	8.6	14.9	3.8	1,197	2,862	4,059	—	41	9	6	160	11,051	1.43
1989	7.9	9.3	17.2	4.8	1,434	3,112	4,596	—	58	9	13	319	20,927	2.61

[1]Rounding explains .1 difference.

[2]1986 total plus 1987 added is 14.2 versus 13.9. This is due to counting rule changes. Also, LOC added is less than LOC activity which counts changed and delted code.

[3]Programs Changed versus Total Programs.

NOTE: LOC from LOC Report plus 15% to account for JCL, MARK IV, and Copylibs.

FIELD DESCRIPTIONS

(A) O/L—On-line installed Lines of Code from automated reporting system in millions

(B) Bat—Batch installed Lines of Code from automated reporting system in millions

(C) Tot (Mil)—Total installed Lines of Code from automated reporting system in millions

(D) LOC Added (Mil)—LOC added during year from automated reporting system (in millions)

(E) O/L—On-line count of programs from automated reporting system

(F) Batch—Batch count of programs from automated reporting system

(G) Total—Total count of programs from automated reporting system

(H) Added Pgms—Number of programs added during year from automated reporting system

(I) Tot Imp—Total projects (75 man-days and greater) installed during the calendar year

	UCRs												STAFFING		
	TOT UCRS	NO CHG 40/1	MAJ CHG 42	MIN CHG 43	JCL 44/8	COR 45	STDS 46	S/T 49	FPTS	INFO CNTR FPTS	INFO CNTR M/D	SUPP (SB)	SUP	PRJ	TOT
	O	P	Q	R	S	T	U	V	W	X	Y	Z	AA	BB	CC
1982	1,107	258	162	102	427	87	47	—	19,479	—	—	22.7%	118	118	236
1983	1,243	277	144	204	445	66	99	35	18,064	5,516	—	23.3%	128	92	220
1984	1,054	290	131	148	383	54	48	50	10,586	3,103	760	32.2%	130	97	227
1985	1,292	336	265	181	382	73	55	71	23,747	8,395	1,234	35.6%	130	101	231
1986	1,279	428	166	192	379	71	43	19	15,160	12,529	1,226	38.1%	143	89	232
1987	1,289	401	208	177	388	58	57	58	15,224	17,596	1,563	36.3%	148	90	238
1988	1,392	608	132	219	358	47	29	31	10,863	21,559	1,543	37.3%	154	98	252
1989	1,608	792	290	221	305	—	—	35	18,820	30,156	1,792	38.0%	157	121	278

(J) Proj Late—Number of projects (75 man-days and greater) installed over one month later than planned date as recorded in design document

(K) Over Budg—Number of projects (75 man-days and greater) installed that exceeded man-days estimated in the design phase by 25 percent or greater

(L) Imp UCRs—Implementation UCRs as reported for the Year-End Report; those UCRs incurred in the first 90 days of system operation

(M) MD on Proj—Actual man-days reported for completion of major projects; project man-days divided by 210 to convert to man-years (regardless of the year the effort occurred in)

(N) LOC (Mil)—LOC implemented by projects as counted by project team (includes copylibs, JCL, and changed LOC) in millions

(O) Tot UCRs—Total 40 series UCRs, less 49's

(P–U) 40–46—UCR classification

(V) S/T 49—System Test UCRs

(W) FPTS—Function Points calculated for major projects (over 75 man-days)

(X) Info Cntr FPTS—Function Points calculated manually at completion of Information Center ad hoc requests

(Y) Info Cntr M/D—Actual man-days devoted to completion of Info Center requests

(Z) Supp—Percent of staff working on support, from time-reporting system

(AA) Sup—Staff budgeted for support

(BB) Prj—Staff budgeted for projects

(CC) Tot—Total staff budgeted

APPENDIX B

Profile of One Software Factory

Characteristics are grouped organizationally: Systems Development, MIS Division, and Corporate.

SYSTEMS DEVELOPMENT CHARACTERISTICS

- Objective of Systems Development:

  Contribute to the company profits by effectively designing, programming, implementing, and maintaining profit-generating or cost-cutting computer systems. For new systems, the life cycle has three phases: Feasibility Study (Analysis), Design, and Implementation. Systems Development is responsible for all three phases on production systems.

  One special purpose group in Systems Development is the Information Center, which serves management by providing: quick response to immediate information needs, user consulting on high-level languages, and resources for small, noncorporate systems.

  The department also has a responsibility to coordinate information system plans for all divisions and to assist the Budget Committee each year in selecting a portfolio of DP projects.

- Budgeted Personnel:

Managers	8
Secretaries	3
Project Managers	27
Programmer/Analysts	238
Standards/Productivity Analyst	2
Total	278

- Support Personnel (Development Center):

Training	2
Database	10
Technical Services	16
Communications	3
Total	31

- Project Organization

  Projects are managed by a Systems Development Project Manager with end users interfacing directly with the project team. Personnel on major development have no maintenance responsibility. All programmer/analysts perform both programming and design tasks.

- Quality Control

  Quality is the responsibility of the project team. They perform the system test although users participate in validation.

- Life Cycle Methodology

  A tailored life cycle, evolving over a 10-year period, is used on all projects. Prototyping concepts are an integral part of the methodology.

- Languages

  Over 90 percent of all development is in COBOL, using IBM's CICS for the on-line network.

- Training

  A complete curriculum of technical courses is offered internally.

- Turnover/Stability

  Twelve percent per year; however, half is to internal company departments either in MIS or user community. Programmer/analyst average experience level is over five years.

- Management Stability

  Management personnel and philosophy has been stable for over seven years.

- Environmental Factors

  Each employee has own office (8 by 10 feet) with 5-foot walls. Area is relatively quiet.
- Recruiting

  College graduates majoring in MIS, DP, Computer Science, with interest in business applications fill 90 percent of openings.

MIS DIVISION CHARACTERISTICS

- MIS Responsibility

  Reporting directly to the Senior Operating Officer, responsibilities include: telecommunication, office automation, end-user computing, and department computers.
- MIS Stability

  Same vice president for 10 years.
- Hardware/Operations

  Large IBM mainframes provide subsecond response time, network support, and adequate on-line storage.
- Consulting/Programming Services

  None for mainframe systems; however, utilized for unique hardware on occasion. Less than 1 percent of budget.

CORPORATE CHARACTERISTICS

- Corporate Environment

  Major emphasis on using MIS to improve internal productivity and as a competitive advantage. Funded as an investment rather than expense. Systems are critical to the daily operation of the corporation. Total MIS expense over 2 percent of revenues.
- Corporate Culture

  Conservative but also progressive, industry leader.
- Applications/Stage of Automation

  Highly integrated, centralized, business applications. For example, order entry feeds order processing, which feeds distribution, which feeds billing, which feeds sales.
- Project Justification

  After reviewing proposed projects, top management, using judgement and intuition, selects those supporting corporate objectives. BSP results in a series of meetings involving senior management.

- Charge-back

  None, handled by project justification process.

- End-User Computing

  The majority of ad hoc reporting is performed directly by end users via Mark 4, SAS, or FOCUS. Decision support systems are also in place.

- User Programming of Production Systems

  Corporate direction is to centralize development of production systems. Consequently, few user areas program or maintain production systems.

- User Knowledge, Location

  Generally, sophisticated users who understand MIS capabilities and work directly with project teams. Majority of users are in same physical complex.

Combining these characteristics produces a unique environment, different from other MIS organizations.

APPENDIX C

The Thadhani Curve

RESPONSE TIME DETAIL

The Thadhani curve, first published in 1981 (Thadhani, 1981 No. 4), plots user transactions per hour versus Computer Response Time (CRT) which excludes network delay of about .2 second. The transactions labeled human intensive include 95 percent of all user transactions in a TSO environment. The response time plotted is the average time as viewed by the terminal user for these transactions versus the other 5 percent of transactions labeled computer-intensive. The surprising relationship is that CRT (and SRT) leverages user response time by a factor of 10. A .1 second change results in roughly 1.1 seconds saved per transaction (.1 system plus 1.0 user). Thus, CRT (and SRT) reductions in tenths of seconds are important; they leverage user response time.

Assuming transactions per hour reflect productive work, the graph documents a surprising result: Productivity increases linearly from 180 to 250 transactions per hour as response time improves from 3 seconds to 1 second, but at 1 second, the slope of the graph becomes dramatically steeper with productivity gains from 290 to 400 transactions per hour as SRT improves from .5 seconds to .25 seconds. In one IBM study with engineers using special graphic terminals, transaction rates of 4,000 per hour were documented. This corresponds to .9 seconds between transactions, a believable value, especially if CRT was .1 or .2 seconds.

To determine if the concept was fact or fiction, a study was completed in 1983. During the year, actual CRT averaged .35 seconds for human-intensive transactions (85 percent of all transactions). The conclusions were:

1. The Thadhani curve is realistic; transaction rates do increase dramatically in the subsecond response-time range. Furthermore, the curve can be verified in any TSO environment.
2. The diverse TSO usage in a large-shop environment makes it unrealistic to expect subsecond computer response time for all transactions, but when provided for 85 percent or more of TSO activity (human intensive transactions), productivity will increase dramatically.
3. Service-level objectives and daily monitoring tools are essential to maintain subsecond service.

The study also posed the question: Will transaction rates continue to climb at this rate as CRT approaches zero? Are we, at .35 seconds, approaching a human threshold for system development activity?

From 1983 to 1987, CRT continued to improve as shown in Table C.1. However, unfortunately, the 1987 data did not include

TABLE C.1. Improvement of CRT for human-intensive transactions, 1984 to 1987.

	Human Intensive Transactions Only				*All Trans*
Time Period	*Avg # Trans*	*Avg Trans/Hr*	*% Of Total Trans*	*CRT*	*CRT*
April–Dec, 1984	2,863,320	301	91.3	0.36	1.27
1985	3,517,071	314	91.1	0.24	.85
1986	4,539,871	347	90.4	0.16	.56
1987	4,638,615	*	88.6	0.12	.50

*Invalid hours since terminals connected to multiple systems.

transactions per hour because of technical considerations (a problem existing today, inherent in the way terminals now use multiple systems concurrently).

Comparing the pre-1987 data with the Thadhani curve (Figure C.1) documents a similar trend, as CRT decreases below .6 seconds to .16 seconds, and transactions per hour increase from 301 to 347. The data are not expected to match the Thadhani curve exactly, primarily because our data represent 90.4–91.3 percent of all transactions and the original curve included 95 percent; secondarily, the environments and on-line activities were not identical.

One popular way to obtain SRT is to add an estimate of network delay to CRT. Figure C.2 is an example of subsecond CRT recorded in 15-minute intervals, with an average of .14 seconds for that day. If local terminals are used, the average network delay is about .2 seconds, then SRT is .34 seconds (.14 + .2) for the day, meeting stated service levels. Figure C.3 is a similar report summarized by day, showing commercial business application (IBM's CICS) CRT, which, in our environment, is higher than the TSO CRT.

If SRT is possible in the .2 seconds range (.09 seconds internal, .1 network), is it below the limits of human reaction? According to Walter Doherty and William Pope (1986):

> *We found that subsecond response time, probably down to 0.1 seconds, is important to avoid disrupting the user's rate of work.*

This is based on physical human characteristics involving eye, brain and hand response.

The focus has been on human intensive transactions, a term synonymous with "trivial" or "short," comprising 90 percent of the activity. But how about the other 10 percent, which contains medium and long transactions? Is their response time also important to productivity? To answer these questions, consider how flat the Thadhani curve is beyond the two-to-three second range, not much productivity gain as response time improves from 4 to 3 seconds. Also, since the computer intensive transactions consume greater resources, more capacity is needed to impact response time. Thus, an objective of minimizing response time at the steepest part of the curve produces optimal results.

FIGURE C.1. The Thadhani curve compared with pre-1987 data.

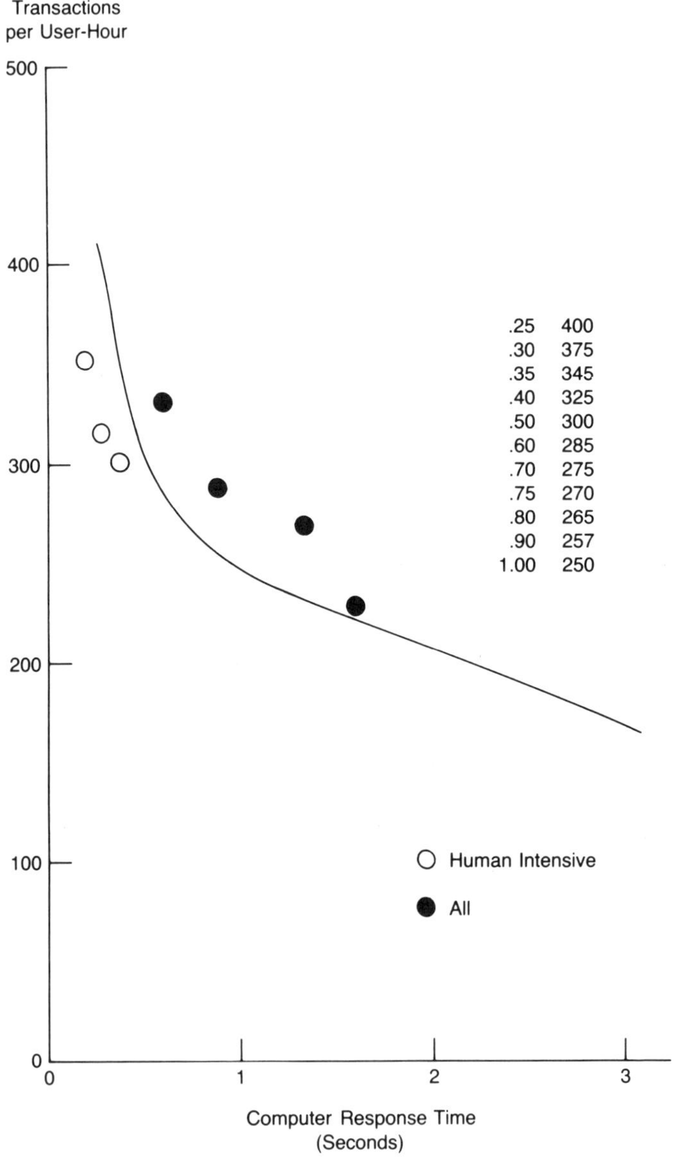

FIGURE C.2. An example of subsecond CRT recorded in 15-minute intervals.

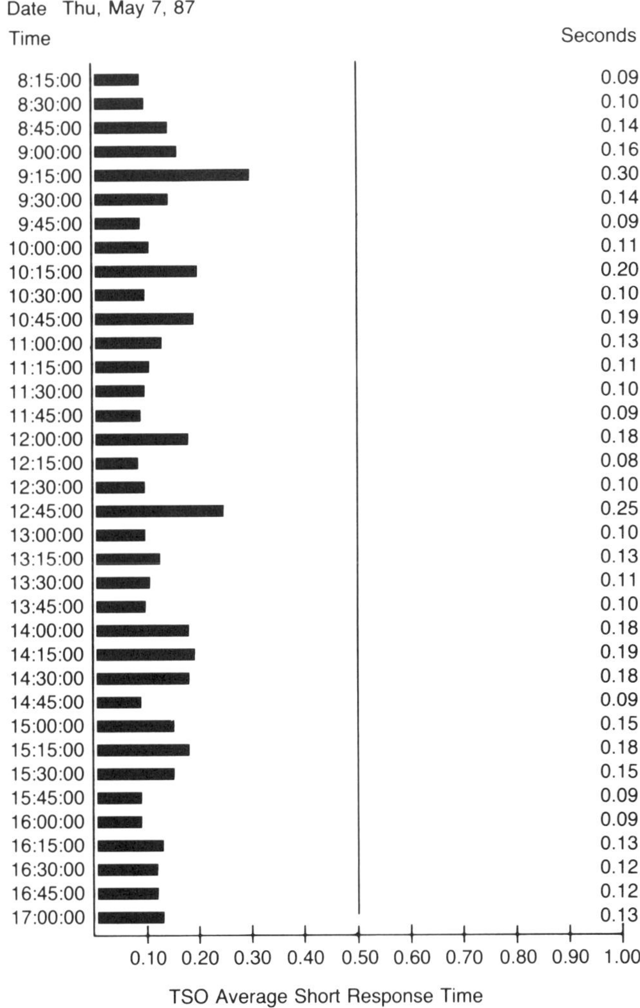

FIGURE C.3. An example of subsecond CRT showing the commercial business CRT.

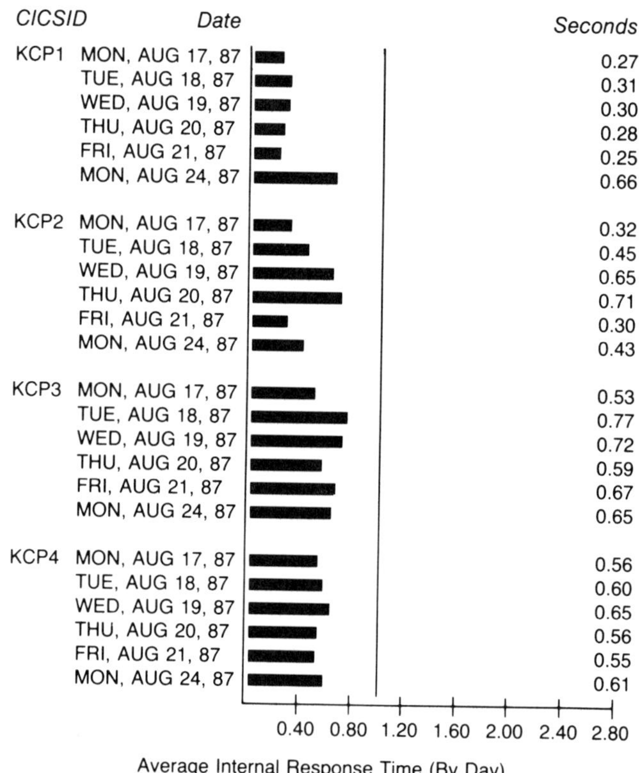

Appendix D

*The Dangers of "Architected" Applications**

A large DP project, designed to replace several existing computer applications with a single, integrated system, takes double the elapsed time planned, almost triple the proposed development budget, and finally consumes 40 MIPS of processing when implemented, when the total of the systems it replaces used 6 MIPS. Most importantly, promised business results are not attained.

The growing frequency of such occurrences should be of major concern to all I/S professionals. Results like this reinforce the impression that, despite technological progress, our ability to successfully apply technology is in trouble. User organizations become dissatisfied with large I/S departments and their approaches, and management concludes that I/S is not a particularly good choice for investment.

Based on the author's experience in conducting project reviews in situations of project difficulty, a change in corporate I/S project patterns has been observed. We are undertaking few projects, but of larger scope, and of increased complexity. Usually,

*Reprinted in condensed version with permission of author (Richard Manicom). Complete text published in Guide 75, Session MP-7064, November 1989.

these are projects designed to replace several existing, old systems, with a stated objective to do a better job while also adopting an "architected" approach to building an "integrated" system. Almost always, we want to modernize both our application development approaches for this new, large project, as well as the technology base our applications run on. Often, the user has asked for nothing except some corrections and enhancements but we conclude, based on a "global architecture study", and supported by the results of modelling activities, that the existing applications must be scrapped in favor of a new system.

Looking at the arguments supporting the conclusion to build a new, integrated system, we see a remarkable consistency of logic used most of the time. After evaluating our existing applications against our ideal view of what we would like, we conclude that they duplicate data, are not integrated, are based on various old technologies, are poorly documented, are difficult to maintain, are not user friendly, and generally do not exploit current technologies such as relational data bases, fourth generation languages, and intelligent workstations. We therefore conclude these applications are unsalvageable and must be scrapped.

The new system, we argue, will be "integrated" (a term we don't define very well), "architected" (which may mean designed without respect for physical constraints), easy to maintain, present a single user interface, and of course use all the latest technology. The new system will be "global", by which we mean it will do everything everyone wants, unlike the existing fragmented systems.

It is not clear how the term "architecture" made it into the application development field, but it should generally be regarded as a warning sign that the analysts intend to back up significantly from the problem to be solved, and take a very high level view, supported by modelling and other techniques, of the real information flows in the business. Backing up from the problem usually results in a broader scope. Data modelling and its related disciplines, unless very tightly managed, result in much richer function and more complex data structures, as well as a way of thinking that encourages specification of requirements without regard for what is feasible, justifiable, and actually needed by the business. All business requirements seen to be subsets of larger problems, and we back up further and further from the specific needs, and broaden the scope of the project beyond what is reasonable.

Our experience causes us to believe current methodologies are a major cause of projects growing in size and scope, with much more functional richness in the delivered application than really necessary, and often unrealistically complex data structures being implemented. In particular, analysts using current methodologies are encouraged to view the problem without reference to physical constraints, with the view that conceptually, anything is possible. Other people downstream in the development process will somehow reduce our specifications into something that will work. Excessive emphasis is placed on the users' statements of needs with little consideration given to what is practical or necessary. As data flows are studied, organizational boundaries are crossed, together with the boundaries of existing, discrete applications, producing the conclusion that multiple existing systems must be scrapped in order to build a single application that looks at all the data without duplication.

It would be unreasonable to place all the blame for these problems on the shoulders of our current methodologies. However, they must take a large share of the responsibility. While there is nothing specific in the data-driven design processes to force the problems I have noted, these methodologies seem to encourage a thought process that results in a lack of realism, excessive idealism, generalization, abstraction, and enlargement of scope.

Analysis of the project results in cases where current methodologies have been diligently pursued suggests that many of the basic principles we currently embrace in theory must be significantly tempered in practice if we expect the project to be of reasonable scope and complexity.

To support this observation, we note that the pattern of reasons for large project failure is changing. Historically, project management ineptitude, failure to understand user requirements, lack of management commitment, and technical problems were the most common reasons for failure. Now, we are seeing less of the first three and more failures due to complexity, size, methodology, and idealism. The technical problems category remains, although it is often unjustly used as the reason for failure. In some cases, millions have been spent implementing an idealistic design that can be shown to be technically impossible due to a single factor: data structure complexity. In this case we all cite technology problems as the cause, but really the issues are idealism, scope, lack of reality, and lack of business justification.

A mid-project crisis usually appears about 30 months into the development of the "global, fully-integrated, architected" system. Millions have been spent, and no user deliverables have been produced. We have models, prototypes, documentation, standards, data base designs, common modules, and interface specifications. The users, who never wanted the "global, integrated system", become impatient. With the extended duration, the statistical probability of a senior management change increases, and when it happens, tough questions are asked about the benefits being received for the millions spent. The users start to time out and seek alternative, departmental-level solutions, and the project is cancelled, often with career implications for the participants.

As more organizations experience the creation of mega-projects, as project failure rates increase, and as unjustifiable costs and levels of complexity are incurred, there will be a change in application development approaches in the 1990s. In particular, there will be a questioning of data driven approaches, and reduced worship of purity of data and of data structure. There will be suspicion of project proposals to integrate applications, where the justification to integrate is based on data processing ideology as opposed to business needs. Instead, organization will evolve their applications with bite-sized projects that work, and are of a manageable degree of risk. There will be more focus on automating business functions, and less on understanding the data for its own sake. There will be a compromise in idealism and design purity in favour of an emphasis on the pragmatic and the justifiable. Hopefully all this will be followed by a return of end user conficdence in the I/S Department, in the technology and methodologies they use, and in their ability to deliver systems that work.

APPENDIX **E**

Lower Case

Code Generators (Lower CASE products) discussed in Chapter 4, provide multilevel facilities to improve productivity.

The productivity pyramid, Figure E.1, illustrates the integrated approach. Productivity is highest when nonprocedural code is used. A simplistic definition of nonprocedural code: Describe what is to be done versus how it is to be done. For example, painting a CRT screen to generate the on-line program or producing a report by checking off the fields needed, selection criteria, sort sequence, rollup, etc. However, many program functions are too complex for the more general nonprocedural language. Thus, an integrated way of inserting macros (reusable parameter-driven code), procedural specifications, and specialized COBOL code is needed. The more "seamless" the integration, the better.

The key to productivity improvements is reusing pre-tested code. When the nonprocedural approach covers 100 percent of the programming, all pre-tested code is used. As a system needs more tailoring or specialized code, macros may apply followed by procedural specifications (an abbreviated COBOL) and finally COBOL, the most popular commercial programming language. Note the productivity ratios at each level which are relative guidelines (Figure E.1).

FIGURE E.1. The productivity pyramid.

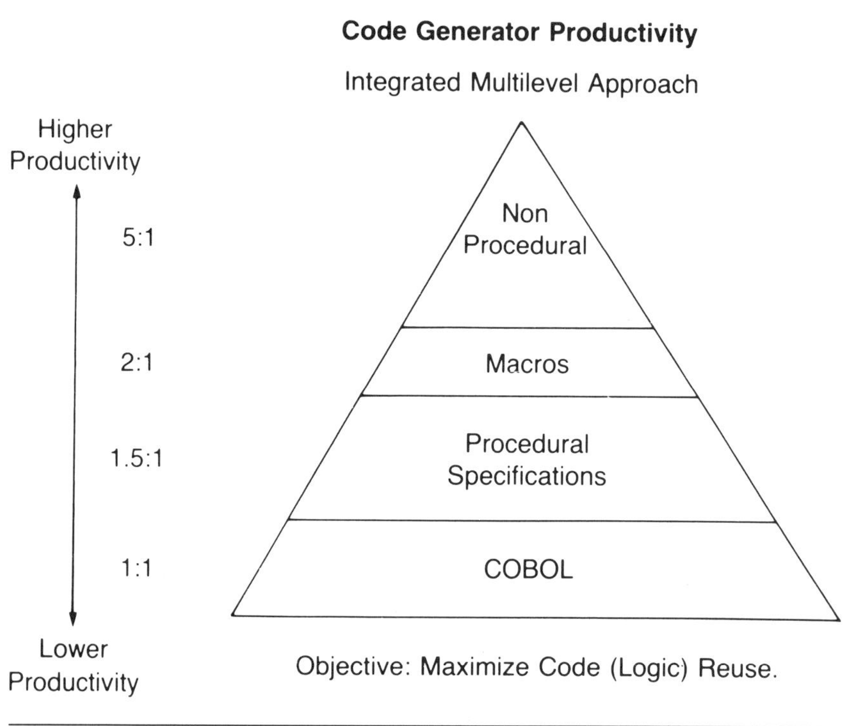

Expanding further on the three types of macros helps explain standardization. The first type of macro is supplied by the vendor. "Integrated," "sophisticated," "comprehensive" best describe their functions. Examples are: database commands (obtain, modify, store, etc.) and CICS commands (send, link, etc.). The second type of macro, the shop macro, is less sophisticated than the first, performing functions such as account validation, screen placement of date, time, terminal ID, etc. The staff internally develops these macros and must be skilled because, by definition, macros perform multiple functions based on parameters passed from the program using the macro. Thus, the writing and testing of macros is a critical function. The more general macros are, typically, the more complex. The third macro type, project macros, are team-specific, developed to eliminate redundant coding. They are simpler than other macros handling special error-processing or unique file access.

Thus, code generators not only provide a nonprocedural approach but also provide techniques to standardize other functions with reusable parameter driven code—macros. Implied with this capability is a dictionary to link screens, programs, reports, macros, etc. The dictionary primarily functions as a communication mechanism, informing project teams what facilities are available.

EVALUATION PLAN

This may not be a surprise, but software evaluation plans have a common format. Consider the following steps:

1. Develop requirements
2. Visit vendors for demos
3. Reduce number of candidates
4. Visit customers using product
5. Visit vendor for "prove it" demo
6. Make product selection
7. Environmental analysis/business case
8. Develop installation plan
9. Install product, begin training
10. Begin pilot project

An evaluation period of 6 to 12 months is required, although many organizations take longer. Comments on selected steps (1, 5, 7, and 10) follow.

Requirements (step 1) define product scope, target environment, performance, and vendor support. Reference Figure E.2 for the general topics in each of these areas. When visiting vendors (step 5), use existing program specifications to test the code generator capabilities. Due to unique technical environments, completing an executable system may not be possible, but understanding the concepts is facilitated with this plan. The economic analysis/ business case (step 7) is the critical cost-justification process. A payback calculation is dependent on purchase price, training and support costs, percent of staff that can use the product, and productivity improvement expected. It may be obvious, but code generators do not impact existing systems immediately. In two or three years, as projects are implemented, the productivity increase for maintenance is a factor and may be as significant as project productivity. However, since a payback of four or less years is usually required, maintenance may not enter into the calculation. Thus, only staff on new projects or major enhancements should be included. Also, since most code generators have capabilities for both Upper and Lower CASE, the impact on the entire life cycle must be analyzed. Consider these numbers as guidelines for staff impact and productivity:

a. Equivalent staff benefiting	20–30%
b. On-line productivity improvement	25–35%
c. Batch productivity improvement	10–15%

The first factor is a composite consisting of percent new development, impact on life cycle phases, percent nonprocedural coding possible, and macro utilization. Note the higher productivity for on-line versus batch programming. The payback calculation is highly sensitive to these assumptions.

Justification is far easier when a factory is preparing for a major system rewrite or development effort. However, the majority of companies may not have a 20+ man-year effort planned. In this situation, benefits accrue more slowly on enhancements and medium-size projects. The code generator support team—in most situations, one to three staff members—is an overhead expense required to write macros, train, and promote standardization.

The last step, the pilot project, theoretically is required to validate the business case, but this validation is not necessarily conclusive. Pilots are just that, a test case in a constantly changing environment. Our productivity measures, both lines of code (LOC) and function points, show projects varying dramatically based on partially controllable factors: technology, user expertise, complexity, and system interface. Management support and expectation of a pilot may influence the results. And finally, the Hawthorne effect is always present. For these reasons, the decision is based, to some degree, on subjective opinion.

FIGURE E.2. Requirements for code generator.

Product Scope

Significantly increase productivity
Batch and CICS
Development and maintenance
Support prototyping
At least a passive dictionary

Target Environment

Support highly complex applications
Fit existing CICS standards
Create standalone COBOL programs

Performance

Generate efficient COBOL code
User friendly development environment

Vendor Support

Training
Responsive problem resolution

PARADOX/CONCLUSION

A paradox exists with code generators: The productivity promise is great, but the promise (software) has turned to "shelf-ware" (used once, then shelved) in many organizations. Analysis of code generators results in the following conclusions:

a. Significant productivity gains are possible for new development, especially on line.

b. Code generators are the future.

In summary, they allow the transition from typical "job-shop" development, where every product is tailored to an "assembly line" mode of operation where standard parts (macros or blocks of code) are assembled to produce the product.

With this endorsement of the concept, why a paradox? Why have code generators become shelfware in many companies? The root of the paradox is standardization. Implementing standardization (user interfaces and program code) is not popular because personal preferences are involved. One team resists conforming with other teams' conventions when differences do not necessarily enhance system operation. Also, consider the other conclusions:

a. No one product has everything.
b. Products are improving rapidly.
c. Technical support is essential.
d. Maintenance productivity improvements must evolve over many years.

A product without proper training, technical support, and management commitment gradually fades away. However, with proper planning, code generators will improve productivity significantly; they are the future for large, complex, COBOL-based Software Factories.

Appendix **F**

Performance Measures

DISCUSSION OF 1989 RESULTS

This section lists the 1989 results (see Figure F.1) along with the general and specific objectives. The discussion below includes some historic results for comparative purposes. The database supporting the calculations has four components: Lines of Code—an automated system scans source librarians for the majority of counts although project counts were manual; time-reporting hours—a system records work hours against pre-defined tasks either as maintenance, enhancements, or development; Function Points—calculated by project team and validated by Productivity Coordinator; and production problems (UCRs—Unusual Condition Reports or program bugs)—recorded by Data Center Operations.

Productivity Measure One

$$\text{Support Productivity} = \frac{\text{Total LOC}}{\text{Equivalent Support Staff}}$$

The output, Total LOC Supported, provides a measure of system size. The organization adds 1 to 2.5 million LOC per year; thus,

FIGURE F.1. 1989 performance measure results and objectives.

Performance Measure		*General Objective*	*1989 Specific Objective*	*1989 Calculations*	*1989 Actual*
A. PRODUCTIVITY					
1. Support Productivity	$= \frac{\text{Total LOC}}{\text{Equiv Support Staff}}$	Increase	160,000	$\frac{17.2M}{99}$	173,400
2. Project Productivity	$= \frac{\text{Project LOC Implem}}{\text{Project Man-Years}}$	Maintain or Increase	25,000	$\frac{2.61M}{20{,}927/210}$	26,191
3. Function Point Productivity	$= \frac{\text{Function Points}}{\text{Project Man-Days}}$	Increase	.9	$\frac{18820}{20927}$	.90
4. LOC Productivity	$= \frac{\text{LOC Activity}}{\text{Equiv Enhance/Dev Staff}}$	Increase	22,000	$\frac{4.8M}{162}$	29,630
5. Info Center Productivity	$= \frac{\text{Function Pt}}{\text{Programming Man-Days}}$	Increase	12.0	$\frac{30{,}156}{1792}$	16.83
B. QUALITY					
1. Maintenance UCRs	$= \frac{\text{Total LOC}}{\text{Tot UCR Cnt—Proj UCRs}}$	Maintain or Increase	11,000	$\frac{17.2M}{1608 - 319}$	13,344
2. Project UCRs	$= \frac{\text{Project LOC Implem}}{\text{Project UCRs}}$	Maintain or Increase	7,500	$\frac{2.61M}{319}$	8,182
C. ESTIMATING					
1. Schedule Estimate	$= \frac{\text{Projects On or Ahead Schedule}}{\text{Total Projects}}$	Increase	80%	$\frac{49}{58}$	84.5%
2. Budget Estimate	$= \frac{\text{Projects On or Under Budget}}{\text{Total Projects}}$	Increase	80%	$\frac{45}{58}$	77.6%

unless more LOC can be supported per person, the support staff must increase each year (calculated as follows: percent support times total staff minus information center staff). Our general objective is to increase this ratio. Based on previous years' history, the specific objective for 1989 was set at 160,000. The results for 1989 were:

$$\text{Support Productivity} = \frac{17{,}200{,}000}{99} = 173{,}400 \text{ LOC/person}$$

Productivity Measure Two

$$\text{Project Productivity} = \frac{\text{Project LOC Implemented}}{\text{Project Man Years}}$$

To qualify as a project, the effort must be over 75 man-days or have significant corporate visibility. For 1989, the average man-days for 58 projects installed was about 360, or 1.7 man-years. Historically, Project LOC has received considerable criticism; however, if recording rules are consistent and if only one language is used, COBOL in our organization, then LOC is considered a reasonable measure of output. Collection simplicity is one inherent advantage, with no separate calculations needed. In fact, the collection of data may be automated. The LOC definition used for the calculation is as follows:

- All source statements (physical lines) including comments for production programs (excludes conversion and test programs)
- Both batch and on-line programs
- Job Control Language
- For projects, counting each line of changed code as two lines (a small percent of total)
- Counting copylib (data definitions) only once
- Not counting deleted code

In 1986, this ratio increased only 1 percent; from 23,300 in 1985 to 23,544. For the previous three years, the increases were dramatic: 1983, 26.2 percent (14,150 to 17,850); 1984, 16.0 percent (17,850 to 20,700); 1985, 12.6 percent (20,700 to 23,300). Understandably, the management team was reluctant to set a goal above 25,000, a figure over two times what most organizations were reporting in published statistics. Thus, the general and specific goal was set at 25,000 plus. The 1989 results were:

$$\text{Project Productivity} = \frac{2{,}610{,}000}{20{,}927/210} = 26{,}191 \text{ LOC/man-year}$$

Productivity Measure Three

$$\text{Function Point Productivity} = \frac{\text{Function Points}}{\text{Project Man-Days}}$$

Function Points quantify processing in five areas: inputs, outputs, master files, inquiries, and system interfaces. A sixth factor, complexity, modifies the calculated value. These are independent of technology, based on system inputs/outputs representing "goods" or "services" provided.

A detailed description of our approach, which is analogous to IBM's technique (Albrecht and Gaffney, 1983) is documented in an article titled "Measuring Applications Development Performance" (*Datamation,* 1984).

According to Capers Jones' statistics on Function Point rates, the maximum for most organizations is in the range of 65 to 120 per man-year. Assuming a 210 man-day year, this is .31 to .57 Function Points per man-day. As with LOC, our numbers are higher, .9 in 1989. Thus, .9 was established as an obtainable specific goal. The 1989 results were:

$$\text{Function Point} = \frac{18{,}820}{20{,}927} = .90 \text{ Function Points/man-day}$$

Our organization uses Function Points as an after-the-fact measure of output; however, many companies also use Function Points for estimating project scope, quantifying maintenance responsibility, and estimating enhancements. In these situations, a series of Function Point ratios are possible, such as:

Project = Function Point Actual:Function Point Estimate
Maintenance = Function Point Maintained:Staff to Maintain
Enhancement = Function Point Increase:Man-Days

Productivity Measure Four

$$\text{LOC Productivity} = \frac{\text{Lines-of-Code Activity}}{\text{Equiv. Enhance. \& Dev. Staff}}$$

This ratio addressed the enhancement and development activity in the department. Enhancements are tasks less than 75 man-days but not classified as maintenance. Development is project work greater than 75 man-days. Prior to 1987, we did not automatically count changed, added, or deleted lines of code. During 1987, a method was developed to automatically determine these counts. Weighting of the LOC counts is done to reflect the effort needed and to make the counts comparable to project development LOC counts. Each line of a new program is counted as 1. Each line of a deleted program is counted as ½. Each deleted line of an existing program is counted as 1. Each changed or added line in an existing program is counted as 2. The denominator is the sum of enhancement and development time (total staff less information center less support staff). The 1989 results were:

$$\text{LOC Productivity} = \frac{4{,}800{,}000}{162} = \text{29,630 LOC added/person}$$

Since changed LOC were not previously counted and deleted LOC actually reduced the old Net LOC added figure, this ratio increased. The objective was 22,000.

Productivity Measure Five

$$\text{Information Center Prod.} = \frac{\text{Function Points}}{\text{Programming Man-Days}}$$

This measure monitors Information Center ad hoc reporting in Function Points. As previously noted (measure 2), the project Function Point objective was .9 Function Points per man-day. Since writing ad hoc reports from an established database is producing a direct output, the base of Function Points, it should be inherently more productive than building a complete system. The ratios support this logic:

	1989
a. Project Function Points	.90
b. Info Center Function Points	16.83
c. Times greater (b ÷ a)	18.70

The 1989 calculation was:

$$\text{Info Center Prod} = \frac{30{,}158}{1792} = 16.83$$

A note of caution is appropriate at this point. The Information Center also consults with users helping them with complex requests or providing extract files for both host and PC. But the productivity ratio only covers the ad hoc reporting function. Thus, the caution: A productivity measure may modify behavior if management and staff feel their performance is directly related to the ratios.

Quality Measure One

$$\text{Maintenance UCRs} = \frac{\text{Total LOC}}{\text{Total UCR Count - Project UCRs}}$$

Monitoring UCRs occurring in the maintenance environment is the objective of the first quality ratio. Lines of Code per UCR measures the general "operational" quality of a system. This measure concentrates on the support function, which includes production fixes and enhancements smaller than 75 man-days not classified as projects. Only abend situations caused by Systems Development are part of the UCR count. Other causes, such as Operator Error, Equipment Failure, Vendor Operating System Software, etc. are excluded.

For some installations, improving operational quality might

be the primary objective of the performance measurement program; however, our system operational quality was considered more than acceptable over the past few years. For example, in 1985, only one UCR occurred per year for every 11,900 LOC installed. In 1986, this improved to 1 per 12,965 LOC. Thus, the general objective was to hold steady or increase above the 11,000 level. The results for 1989 were:

$$\text{Maintenance UCRs} = \frac{17{,}200{,}000}{1608\text{-}319} = 13{,}344 \text{ LOC/UCR}$$

Quality Measure Two

$$\text{Project UCRs} = \frac{\text{Project LOC Implemented}}{\text{Project UCRs}}$$

The ratio reflects the operational quality of systems and thoroughness of project installation planning. In general, it is desirable to increase the Lines of Code installed per UCR; however, increasing beyond an acceptable level, at the expense of productivity, might not be desirable.

The UCRs were recorded for a three-month period following installation. As expected, more errors occurred per installation than in maintenance. The results from 1989 were:

$$\text{Project UCRs} = \frac{2{,}600{,}000}{319} = 8{,}182 \text{ LOC/UCR}$$

Support lines of code have about half the UCRs of recently installed projects. The 1989 project objective was to exceed 7,500 LOC installed for each UCR.

Estimating Measure One

$$\text{Schedule Estimate} = \frac{\text{Projects On or Ahead of Schedule}}{\text{Total Projects}}$$

In this calculation, a project was considered late if it was 20 work days over the date established prior to the implementation phase. A specific goal of 80 percent was selected for 1989. The results:

$$\text{Schedule Estimate} = \frac{49}{58} = 84.5\%$$

When completing projects on time is the primary goal, poor corporate decisions may result. For example, delaying known system enhancements may keep the project on schedule but cost significantly more to add after installation.

Estimating Measure Two

$$\text{Budget Estimate} = \frac{\text{Projects On or Under Budget}}{\text{Total Projects}}$$

Budget overruns consume resources and may create credibility gaps. Thus, a performance measure is needed. For a project to qualify as over budget, the implementation must exceed the man-day estimate by 25 percent. This reflects a philosophy of tight estimating, not padding the effort with excessive unknown factors. Also estimating, especially when modifying existing systems, is subjective, and most managers are forever optimistic. The goal for 1989 was 80 percent.

The Results:

$$\text{Budget Estimate} = \frac{45}{58} = 77.6\%$$

As mentioned previously, each organization has unique opportunities for improving its operation with performance measures. For us, sustaining current levels with gradual improvements was the primary objective. Other organizations in the lower ranges of output, as compared with national statistics, may desire to double productivity in a three-year period. Ratios similar to those described would apply in these situations.

Index

U

W

Z